Kids in the KITCHEN

Kids
in the
KITCHEN

70+ Fun Recipes for Young Chefs to Stir Up!

Rossini Perez

ROCK
POINT

INTRODUCTION

BREAKFAST

29

SNACKS

107

DESSERTS

133

LUNCH

55

DINNER

81

SMOOTHIES & FRUIT JUICES

159

INTRODUCTION

Hello, my name is Rossini Perez. I am a foodie and mother all rolled into one. I combine my love for my children and for food to make creative and fun kid- and family-friendly meals.

I come from a Dominican family where we would usually eat the same variations of foods for breakfast, lunch, and dinner throughout the week. When I was younger, I so looked forward to our weekend outings when we would get "outside" food. I remember when I was old enough to cook for myself, I would make the most random combinations (such as Chef Boyardee with an egg on top), and I just thought I was making the most creative meal ever. I felt so proud. And that's where my love for food started.

Although I have always loved food, when I became a mother and my daughter moved on from baby foods, I found myself struggling with keeping her interested in foods or even trying out new foods. Slowly, I began to let myself become more free with food. I started using colors and playful food ideas to pique her interest. As the years have passed and my daughter and family have grown, so has my brand, Tina Takes Lunch. Parents and non-parents enjoy the ideas that I share, while learning to accept all kinds of foods in a balanced way.

As a teacher by trade, I have no formal cooking training, and my experience comes from years of parenting. I have found that many of us have the same struggles when it comes to feeding children. My goal is to show you, parents and kids alike, that food can be fun and creative but also nutritious and balanced. Teaching children how to cook is a valuable life skill and it's one of the best ways to teach them about nutrition and food safety, as well as build math, science, literacy, and fine motor skills.

I started posting kids, lunch videos on Instagram under the name Tina Takes Lunch as a way to document different ways I could serve my daughter the foods that she enjoyed. At first, I kept the lunches pretty basic, but soon I realized that food can also be creative. Why can't heart strawberries go in a lunchbox? Who makes the rules for making lunch? And right then is when Tina Takes Lunch was born. By being creative and continuously exposing my daughter to new foods, I have helped her become a curious eater, always willing to at least try something.

For the last couple of summers, my daughter has been learning how to cook for herself and most recently for the family. After every meal, she is so happy and fulfilled. Hopefully, your child (if you are a parent reading this) or you (if you are the child reading this) will feel the same way after completing any of the recipes in this book.

KITCHEN RULES

Here are some simple rules to follow as you work your way through the kitchen.

1. **Practice kitchen safety.** This is an absolute must when working with hot things such as stoves, ovens, slow cookers, and air fryers, as well as when working with sharp items such as knives. Even if you have some experience in the kitchen, it's always good to ask for help and have an adult present to assist you when needed.

2. **Avoid cross-contamination.** Do not let food items that you have to cook, such as chicken or pork, touch other foods that you will be eating or don't need to cook, such as salads or raw veggies. When preparing raw foods that need to be cooked, don't use the same utensils for other food items (e.g., don't use the same cutting board you used to cut raw chicken to then cut a carrot). Be sure to properly clean and sanitize utensils before using them for another food item.

3. **Wash your hands.** It is recommended that you wash your hands with soap for at least 20 to 30 seconds. Washing your hands avoids cross-contamination and spreading germs. Always wash your hands before you start working with food, before serving others or yourself, and when dealing with raw food (especially any raw meats, poultry, or eggs).

4. **Wash your veggies and fruits.** Wash your vegetables and fruits before consuming or cooking them, so you remove any harmful chemicals or bacteria from them. However, you don't want to necessarily do that with your meats. The USDA Food and Safety Inspection Service recommends you do not wash your meats because it increases the risk of cross-contamination and foodborne illnesses.

5. **Stay focused and read through instructions carefully.** Read through the recipes before you start and as many times as you need to ensure you understand them and know what ingredients and equipment you require. Keep in mind that some recipes have time ranges (e.g., cook until lightly brown for 8 to 10 minutes) that account for various stove-top options and temperatures. Start with the lower time range, and if the food is not done, keep cooking until it is. However, once something is overcooked, there is nothing you can do. Make sure that anything that is raw is fully cooked before consuming it, such as chicken or pork; when in doubt, you can use a thermometer to check whether something is cooked properly. See pages 23 to 24 for internal temperatures and how to use a thermometer.

6. **Clean up after yourself.** Be sure to clean up utensils once you are done using them, wipe down and disinfect countertops, and put tools and ingredients away once done. This will ensure less mess and less confusion in the kitchen.

7. **Season your food.** Tasty food requires seasoning. Be sure to at least add some salt and black pepper (preferably freshly cracked using a pepper grinder) to your food. Taste is a matter of preference, so you may want more or less salt and pepper added to the recipes than is called for. And most importantly, taste your food before you serve it.

8. **Have fun!** Cooking is all about being creative in the kitchen (responsibly, of course!). Don't be afraid to try out different things or make some recipes your own. Also, remember that mistakes are completely okay and will most likely happen. Not all of the things you cook will look amazing or taste amazing; sometimes all it takes is practice. It happens to all of us, so don't let it discourage you from experimenting.

KNIFE SAFETY

Choosing the right knife for your hand is important so that you're able to work with it correctly and safely. Below are rules to follow when working with knives.

1. **Hold knives using their handles.** Always hold a knife by the handle. Never hold a knife by the blade, even if the blade looks dull or the knife is small.

2. **Use the right knife for what you are doing.** If you are cutting a small fruit like a grape or a strawberry, you'd want to use a small knife such as a paring knife, but if you are cutting something larger like a pineapple or chicken, you'd want to use a bigger knife.

3. **Always cut away from the body.** Make sure the blade is facing away from your body or anyone else working with you in the kitchen. This limits the possibility of accidentally cutting yourself or others.

4. **Use a flat surface such as a cutting board.** When you are cutting ingredients, always work on a flat surface. This also helps avoid accidents because it keeps the food in one place so that the knife doesn't slip from your fingers.

5. **Use caution when cleaning your knives.** Make sure that you are being safe while cleaning the blades, and store them in a safe place.

NOTE

In this book, each recipe will have different levels of difficulty using the below oven-mitt images. Although the mitts are blue below, the color of the mitts will change depending on the chapter you are in.

= easy recipe   = medium recipe   = advanced recipe

PANTRY MUST-HAVES

Here is a list of basic must-haves for any good chef to have in their kitchen.

CANNED GOODS

- Beans (chickpeas, black, red, etc.)
- Salsa
- Tomato paste
- Tomatoes
- Tuna
- Olives or capers
- Chicken broth
- Roasted red peppers
- Chiles
- Anchovy fillets or paste
- Vegetables
- Fruits
- Mustards
- Hot sauce

RICE & GRAINS

- White rice (can be long or medium)
- Brown rice
- Bread crumbs
- Dried pasta (spaghetti, lasagna, penne, rigatoni, fettuccine, orzo, couscous)
- Polenta
- Oats
- Cornmeal
- Lentils
- Tortillas

FLOURS

- Unbleached all-purpose white
- Whole wheat
- Cake
- Almond or other nut flour

SWEETENERS

- Granulated sugar
- Brown sugar
- Confectioners' sugar
- Maple syrup
- Honey
- Agave syrup or light corn syrup

VINEGARS & OILS

- Extra-virgin olive oil
- Canola or vegetable oil
- Apple cider vinegar
- Red wine vinegar
- Balsamic or sherry vinegar
- Rice vinegar
- White wine vinegar

BAKING INGREDIENTS

- Baking powder
- Pure vanilla extract
- Cocoa powder (unsweetened)
- Cornstarch
- Baking soda (safe for cooking)
- Dry yeast
- Chocolate chips or bars
- Evaporated milk
- Condensed milk

SEASONINGS & HERBS

- Salt (kosher or fine)
- Black pepper
- Bay leaves
- Oregano
- Thyme
- Adobo
- Granulated garlic
- Onion powder
- Seasoned salt
- Curry powder
- Ground cinnamon
- Ground cloves
- Paprika
- Rosemary

NUTS & DRIED FRUITS

- Peanuts
- Almonds
- Hazelnuts
- Pecans and walnuts
- Raisins
- Cranberries
- Apricots
- Dates
- Figs

VEGETABLES

- Potatoes
- Onions
- Garlic
- Shallots

TOOLS AND EQUIPMENT

Every chef needs tools and equipment for cooking. Here is a list of all the tools you will need for the recipes in this book.

- Baking sheets
- Glass measuring cup
- Measuring cups and spoons
- Small, medium, and large bowls
- Large cutting board
- Large platter
- Knife
- Cutting board
- Small, medium, and large skillets

- Spatula
- Muffin pan
- Waffle iron
- Air fryer
- 9 x 13-inch (23 x 33 cm) baking dish
- 5 x 5-inch (13 x 13 cm) baking dish
- 10 x 15-inch (25 x 38 cm) baking dish
- 8 x 8-inch (20 x 20 cm) baking dish

- Food processor
- Large saucepan
- Toothpicks
- Mandoline vegetable peeler
- Stand mixer
- Hand mixer
- Whisk

KITCHEN TALK

Cooking has a language of its own, so here are some essential terms to know.

A

Al dente – An Italian term that means "to the tooth." It refers to the ideal consistency of cooked pasta—when the pasta is tender yet firm to the bite (not mushy or too hard).

Arrange – To place in a certain order.

Assemble – To group together.

B

Batch – To cook in larger amounts.

Beat – To stir rapidly with a mixer to combine ingredients together.

Boil – To heat water or cooking liquid until it bubbles. You usually cook veggies and pasta in boiling water.

Broil – To cook under direct heat, such as the broiler in the oven, to crisp or brown the top of food.

C

Chop – To cut food into small pieces, usually similar in size.

- Chopped fine: Usually ⅛-inch (3 mm) pieces
- Chopped: ¼-inch (6 mm) pieces
- Chopped coarse: ¾-inch (2 cm) pieces

Combine – To stir two or more ingredients together until they are mixed. You can also beat on a mixer on low speed.

Crack – To break an eggshell to remove the egg inside.

Cross-contamination – When bacteria is transferred from one object or substance to another. In cooking, bacteria can be transferred from one food item to another, and it usually happens when working with raw meat. You can get sick from cross-contaminated food.

Cut – To divide into pieces using a knife.

D

Dice – To cut food into cubes of a specific size.

Dip – To put something into a liquid. Can also be a dipping sauce.

Divide – To separate into parts.

Drain – To remove or pour liquid from food using a strainer.

Drizzle – To slowly pour a thin liquid over a food item, such as drizzling chocolate over a strawberry. This is usually done at the end of a recipe to make the recipe look good or give it a hint of flavor.

G

Grate – To shred food into small pieces using a tool like a grater.

Grease – To use a fat such as butter, oils, or nonstick cooking spray to coat a baking sheet or pan to prevent food from sticking to them.

L

Let rest or let cool – To let your food stand at room temperature until it's no longer hot to the touch. This can take up to 15 minutes depending on the food.

M

Melt – To heat solid food on the stove top or microwave until it becomes a liquid, such as melting butter.

Mince – To chop something into tiny pieces, about ⅛-inch (3 mm) pieces or smaller.

Mix – To combine two or more ingredients together. This is a general term that can include stirring, blending, creaming, binding, whipping, and folding.

P

Parchment paper – A greaseproof or grease-resistant, odorless, and tasteless paper that is used to line a pan or to wrap foods in for cooking.

Peel – To remove the skin or rind from a fruit or vegetable.

Pinch – The tiny bit you pick up of a ground substance (typically salt and other spices) between the tip of your index finger and your thumb.

Pipe – To decorate food with frosting, whipped cream, or another mixture using a pastry bag.

Pot – A deep container used to cook stews, soups, and other large portions of food.

Pour – To transfer liquid from one container to another or into or over something.

Preheat – To make something hot before you begin cooking. Usually you preheat an oven before cooking food in it.

R

Reduce – To simmer or boil a liquid until some of the water evaporates and the liquid thickens, causing the flavor to intensify.

Roll out – To flatten food, usually dough or pastry, using a rolling pin.

S

Saucepan – A deep pan with a long handle and a top. This type of pan is deeper than a sauté pan or frying pan but shallower than a stockpot.

Sauté – To cook food in a small amount of fat over high heat while tossing the ingredients around.

Seal – To close food, such as pie dough, so that the items inside don't spill while cooking.

Season to taste – To add seasonings such as salt and black pepper to your personal taste preference.

Shred – To cut or tear into small, long, narrow pieces.

Sift – To pass an ingredient such as flour through a sieve to break up lumps.

Simmer – To cook a liquid just below the boiling point (212°F or 100°C) and cook at a range of 185°F (85°C) to 205°F (96°C).

Slice – To cut food with a knife into thin and uniform pieces.

Stir – To mix food with a spoon in a circular motion.

T

Tender – Cooking until the food has become soft enough to cut into or eat.

Toast – To heat food, usually bread, in a toaster, skillet, or oven until golden brown.

Toss – To lightly mix ingredients so as not to damage their shape or texture, such as tossing a salad with dressing.

Transfer – To move a food item from one place to another, such as from a baking sheet to a wire rack.

W

Whip – To combine food vigorously with a whisk, hand mixer, or stand mixer to incorporate air and increase the volume, such as for whipped cream.

Whisk – To blend ingredients together quickly using a wire whisk or fork, or to blend to incorporate air and increase the volume, such as for egg whites or heavy cream.

Z

Zest – To remove the outer rind of citrus fruits, such as oranges, lemons, and limes, to use in cooking.

HOW TO SEASON PROPERLY

Seasoning your food is all about improving the flavors with spices, seasonings, and herbs, usually with at least the addition of salt and black pepper. Throughout this book, some recipes will ask you to season to taste, and that means you should season according to your taste buds. Most of the recipes here use salt and pepper, but you can use any spice, seasoning, or herbs that make sense and taste good! Check out your pantry must-haves (see page 10) for example seasonings, spices, and herbs to have in your kitchen. Some of my personal favorite spices are adobo, garlic powder, onion powder, and oregano.

But first, let's begin with how to season properly. How do you season your food? Well, start by adding some salt to give the food some taste. There are many kinds of salts, but the most common are fine, kosher, and sea salt. What is the difference? Fine salt has much smaller grains and has a more complex flavor profile than kosher salt, which has a more neutral flavor and larger crystals. Fine salt carries more sodium than kosher salt. Sea salt can come in many varieties and can be coarser like kosher salt or smaller grains like fine salt. It does carry a saltier flavor than kosher or fine salt and is typically used to finish a dish. You can use any of these salts to season your food. Let's also talk about another major seasoning that most people use, which is black pepper. Freshly ground pepper lends more flavor than your typical pre-ground pepper, so if you can, use freshly ground pepper over pre-ground.

Make sure that as you are adding your seasonings you are moving your food around to fully coat the food. You want to also taste your food to check the seasoning—be sure the food is safe (fully cooked) to eat, of course. Tasting your food as you are cooking and getting a sense of the flavor will help you decide how much seasoning to add. Always start seasoning with small measurements (such as a sprinkle or a pinch) before deciding to add more. You can always add more flavor, but once something is too salty, you can't go back.

HOW TO PREP YOUR KITCHEN FOR COOKING

Prepping your ingredients and yourself before starting to cook is essential in any kitchen. Here are some quick tips to get started.

1. Read the recipe from start to finish and make sure that you understand it.

2. Be sure that you have all of the ingredients on hand or any substitutions that you can work with.

3. Make sure you have all the equipment you will need or any substitutions you can work with.

4. Always start out with a clean kitchen (e.g., no dishes in the sink, clear and sanitized countertops).

5. Wash your hands and look at which ingredients in the recipe call for you to prep them beforehand. In the following sections, I'll touch on ingredients that need prepping.

WASHING FRESH PRODUCE

Always wash produce properly. While there is a debate on the best way to do this, the FDA recommends using just water to wash fruits and vegetables. Here's how:

1. Follow the steps for how to prep your kitchen (above), then wash any fruits with peels such as oranges and lemons before cutting into them to avoid any cross-contamination into the inside of the food.

2. Cut away any rotting or bruised parts of the produce.

3. If you are working with firmer fruits like apples or lemons and veggies like potatoes and carrots, rinse them with water and brush with a clean, soft-bristle brush.

4. For leafy green vegetables like lettuce and spinach, remove the outermost layer and then place them in a bowl of cold water for 2 to 3 minutes. Once they have soaked for a bit, lift them out of the water, leaving any grit in the bottom of the bowl, and rinse them again with fresh water.

5. With more delicate fruits such as berries, rinse them under a steady stream and gently use your hands to clean them.

PREPARING CITRUS FRUITS

If you will be zesting and juicing a fruit, always zest it first before cutting and juicing.

* To zest citrus fruits, use a rasp grater to remove the skin (or zest). Keep turning the fruit as you zest it to avoid the white layer underneath. This layer is bitter!

* To juice citrus fruits, cut the fruit in half and then use a juicer or your hand to squeeze the halved fruit over a bowl and remove the juice. If any seeds fall into the bowl, use a spoon or strainer to remove them.

MELTING BUTTER

Butter is usually easiest to melt using a microwave, especially if a recipe asks you to add melted butter while you are already cooking the recipe. You can also melt butter in a pan. I recommend doing this when you need to melt butter before cooking your food in the same pan, to prevent the food from sticking to the pan. If the butter is to be added later in the recipe, then microwaving is the easiest option. Cut the butter into uniform pieces and place in a microwave-safe bowl. Place the bowl in the microwave for 30 to 45 seconds (or as needed until the butter melts). Use oven mitts when removing the hot bowl from the microwave.

MINCING GARLIC

While most recipes in this book call for garlic cloves, it's important to know how to mince garlic. To do this, crush garlic cloves with the bottom of a measuring cup to loosen the papery skin so it's easier to remove. Peel carefully using your fingers. If the peel is still not budging, you can use a small knife to help. Once peeled, place the garlic on a cutting board. Place one hand on the handle of your knife and the other on the top of the blade and begin to chop finely (into thin slices), making sure to trim the edges of each clove. You might find that some garlic pieces get stuck to your knife as you are cutting, so carefully wipe the sides of your knife between cuts.

SHREDDING OR GRATING CHEESE

When shredding or grating cheese, keep your hand safely away from the sharp edges and holes of the box grater. If you're an adult working with a younger child, it might be a good idea to have your toddler use cut-resistant cooking gloves.

* To shred cheese, use the large holes on the box grater to make longer pieces. The most common shredded cheeses are softer cheeses such as mozzarella and cheddar.

* To grate cheese, use the smaller holes on the box grater or a rasp grater to make small pieces. Some cheeses that are commonly grated include Parmesan and Parmigiano Reggiano, among others.

HOW TO CHOP INGREDIENTS

The most common vegetables you will chop in this book are fresh herbs, onions, carrots, russet potatoes, peppers, and broccoli. Ask an adult for help when in doubt!

FRESH HERBS

1. Wash and dry your herbs using a clean kitchen towel or paper towel.
2. Make sure you are using the proper knife so that you can control it well. Also make sure the knife is sharp enough to cut.
3. Use your hands to remove the leaves from the stems.
4. Discard the stems and gather all of the leaves together.
5. Place one hand on the handle of the knife and rest the other on the top of the blade as you chop.
6. Chop into the size called for in the recipe.

ONIONS

1. Cut the onion in half with a knife and use your hands to remove the skin.
2. Place the flat end of the halved onion on your cutting board and make vertical cuts from the root end. This will give you slices.
3. Rotate your onion and slice across the vertical cuts; you will end up with a diced onion.

CARROTS

Carrots can be tricky to cut as they tend to roll. Keep a firm grip on your carrots and if you are cutting large carrots, you may want to cut them into two or three pieces before cutting to your desired shape or size. Here are four basic ways you can cut carrots: julienne, baton, diced, and shredded.

Julienne

1. Wash your carrots and pat them dry with a clean kitchen towel or paper towel.
2. If the skin looks rough, peel it off using a peeler.
3. Working on a cutting board, place one hand on the handle of your sharp knife and the other on the carrot to hold the carrot steady. Keep your hand safely away from the blade of your knife. Cut off the ends of the carrots.

4. Cut a thin slice off one side of the carrot, then place the carrot on this side. This helps keep the carrot steady as you slice.

5. Cut the length of the carrot into thin slices (about ⅛ inch [3 mm] thick). Stack all of the thin slices on top of each other and cut lengthwise again. Then cut across the long sticks to make smaller matchsticks.

Baton

1. Follow steps 1 through 4 of the julienne method.

2. Cut the carrot into two to four equal-size pieces, each 2 to 3 inches (5 to 7.5 cm) long.

3. Cut the length of the carrots into slices (the thickness will depend on what the recipe calls for, or your preference). Stack all of the slices on top of each other and cut lengthwise again to the same thickness as the first cut.

Diced

1. Follow steps 1 through 3 of the baton method.

2. Cut across the sticks into equal-size dice.

Shredded

1. Use your less-dominant hand to hold your carrot and your dominant hand to peel using a vegetable peeler. Peel the outer layers of the carrot.

2. Shred the lower part first then the upper part of the carrot.

RUSSET POTATOES

1. Wash your potatoes and pat them dry using a clean kitchen towel or paper towel.

2. Peel your potatoes using a peeler or a paring knife. Peeling helps make cuts a little cleaner. If you are making a stew and don't want to peel the potatoes, it's not totally necessary, but I do recommend peeling for easier and cleaner cuts.

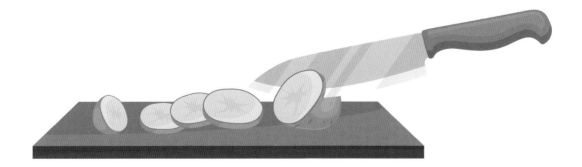

3. Working on a cutting board, place one hand on the handle of your knife and the other on the potato. Keep your hand safely away from the blade of your knife. Cut the potatoes in half.

4. Place the flat side of the potatoes on your cutting board, then cut vertically, cutting your halves into halves.

5. Turn the pieces on their sides and cut vertically again until you have made sticks. (If you are making French fries, you can stop at this step.)

6. If you want to dice the potatoes, cut across the strips to your desired thickness or what the recipe calls for.

BELL PEPPERS

1. Wash your peppers and pat them dry with a clean kitchen towel or paper towel.

2. Working on a cutting board, place one hand on the knife handle and the other on the top of the pepper. The pepper should be standing with the green stem at the top. Slice the bell pepper in half all the way down, through the stem end.

3. Cut around the stem and core, removing and discarding both.

4. Trim the white membrane of the pepper and discard this.

5. Lay the pepper halves cut sides up and slice lengthwise into long vertical strips.

6. Gather all your strips together and cut across them to dice.

BROCCOLI

1. Wash your broccoli and pat dry with a clean kitchen towel or paper towel.

2. Place the head of the broccoli upside down on a cutting board.

3. Place one hand on the handle of the knife and the other on the top of the florets of broccoli. Cut off the stems from the broccoli, right where each floret meets the stem.

4. Slice the large florets into smaller pieces. Start out by cutting them in half vertically, then keep cutting until satisfied with the size.

5. Cut ⅛ inch (3 mm) from each side of the stems to remove the tough outer layer. Slice the stems vertically into ¼-inch (6 mm) pieces.

HOW TO GARNISH AND USE TOPPINGS

Garnishing is the last thing that you do in a recipe to make your dish look appealing. It often includes adding toppings such as sprinkles, berries, herbs, olive oil, or chocolate, to name a few. Here are a few things to take into consideration when garnishing or adding toppings into your dish:

* Consider the color of the dish. It's best to pick a color for your garnish that is different than the color of the dish so that it stands out and helps elevate the dish.

* The garnish or topping should complement the dish well. For example, you wouldn't add minced cilantro to the top of a cheesecake.

* Don't pile on a lot of toppings or garnishes that drown out the main dish. Spread garnishes and toppings lightly and evenly on top of your dish.

* Be creative with patterns and shapes. For instance, adding a straight line of sprinkles on top of a cupcake may not be as appealing as perhaps adding a swirl of sprinkles or a balloon shape.

HOW TO PREPARE DIFFERENT TYPES OF EGGS

There are several styles of eggs you can make depending on your preference or who you are cooking for. From cooking breakfast to making dessert, the egg is the most versatile ingredient in your kitchen. You can use eggs in just about anything, which is why it is important for any chef to know how to cook them. The simplest method is to make a hard-boiled egg. You can also make fried or scrambled eggs, or an omelet.

CRACKING EGGS

First things first, let's talk about how to crack an egg. To work with and cook eggs you have to know how to crack them. So how do you do this?

1. Get a small or medium bowl to place your eggs in.

2. Gently hit the side of the egg against a flat surface like a counter top or a plate.

3. Then, pull the shell apart softly until the egg drops into the bowl.

SEPARATING EGGS

There are recipes (not in this book) that you may find throughout your cooking journey that will ask you to separate the yolk (the yellow part) from the white or clear part of the egg and use them differently in a recipe. Here is how to do this.

1. Get two different small or medium-size bowls.

2. Crack your eggs into one bowl and set your second bowl aside.

3. Use your hand to very gently separate the yolk from the white part of the egg and place the separated yolk into the second bowl.

HARD-BOILED EGGS

1. Fill a medium saucepan with water and bring the water to a boil over medium heat, about 5 minutes.

2. Once boiling, place your eggs in the pan. For this step, it would be helpful to have a steamer basket to lower the eggs safely into the pan, but if not, a soup ladle will work to put in each egg one at a time. You can also ask an adult for help with this.

3. Cover the saucepan and reduce the heat to medium-low. Cook the eggs for 13 to 15 minutes.

4. While the eggs are cooking, combine 2 cups (280 g) of ice and 2 cups (480 ml) of cold water in a large or medium bowl.

5. Use a slotted spoon, soup ladle, or ask an adult to help you remove the eggs and transfer them to the cold water. Let sit for 5 minutes in the water, then remove them, crack them against a hard surface such as a counter top, and peel away the shell. If the egg still feels a little warm, keep dipping it into the cold water as you peel.

FRIED EGGS

There are different types of doneness to enjoy fried eggs, from easy (with lots of runny yolk) to medium (some runny yolk) to hard (solid yolk). Here are the steps to follow to fry your eggs to your liking.

1. In a nonstick skillet, heat 1 tablespoon (15 ml) vegetable oil or butter over low heat.

2. Crack 1 or 2 eggs into the pan. Cook for 1 minute on each side for a runny yolk, for 2 minutes on each side for a medium yolk, and 3 minutes or longer for a hard yolk.

SCRAMBLED EGGS

Scrambled eggs can be a fun way to try out different seasonings. You can add a dash of adobo, salt, black pepper, garlic powder, or onion powder to give these a bit of flavor.

1. In nonstick skillet over medium-low heat, spray nonstick cooking spray or add 1 tablespoon (15 ml) butter.

2. Crack the eggs into the pan. You can add a dash of your preferred seasoning.

3. Stir the eggs with a spatula until they have combined and clumped together, about 2 to 3 minutes.

OMELET

Omelets are fun and easy to make. You can fill an omelet with various ingredients, such as bacon, cheese, spinach, bell peppers, ham cubes, mushrooms, cherry tomatoes, and onions. Here are some simple steps to follow to create your very own omelet.

1. Crack 2 or 3 eggs into a medium bowl and beat them lightly with a spatula or fork for 1 to 2 minutes.

2. In a nonstick skillet, melt 1 to 2 tablespoons (14 to 28 g) butter over medium-low heat, then slowly add your eggs.

3. Reduce the heat to low and let the eggs cook for 1 minute, then use a heatproof spatula to lift the cooked parts of the eggs from the edges of the pan, tilting the pan a bit to allow the uncooked parts to run underneath and cook.

4. Add your favorite fillings to one side of the egg. Be careful not to overfill or the egg might not fold correctly and may break.

5. Fold the bare side of the eggs over the fillings using your heatproof spatula and allow to cook for at least 1 minute before gently flipping to the other side to cook for 1 minute.

6. Add your favorite toppings, such as shredded cheese, avocado, and parsley.

HOW TO COOK DIFFERENT MEATS TO DESIRED DONENESS

The best way to know that a particular meat is cooked is to ensure that it reaches a certain internal temperature. I recommend using a food thermometer to measure the internal temperature of meat. Different types of meat require different degrees of internal temperature. Some meats, such as steaks and burgers, have different levels of doneness depending on personal preference.

STEAKS

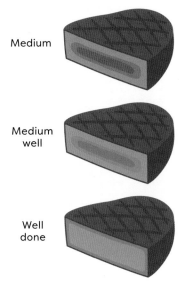

Medium

Medium well

Well done

* Medium (145°F or 63°C) – A medium steak has no red in the center and is mostly pink throughout.

* Medium well (150°F or 66°C) – A medium-well steak is slightly pink in the center.

* Well done (160°F or 71°C) – A well-done steak doesn't have any pink or redness.

While the different level of doneness is a matter of preference, rare steaks or steaks with pink or red centers come with a higher risk of harmful bacteria reaching dangerous levels. The FDA recommends that your steak be at the internal temperature of at least 140°F or 60°C to be safe to eat.

BURGERS AND OTHER MEATS

* Medium (145–150°F or 63–66°C) – This burger is seared on the outside and has a pink center with some slight redness.

* Medium well (150–155°F or 66–68°C) – This burger is seared on the outside, slightly pink in the center, and is mostly cooked throughout.

* Well done (160°F+ or 71°C+) – This burger is seared outside, has no pink, has a fully brown center, and is cooked throughout.

While meats like burgers and steaks have different levels of doneness that depend on personal preference, meats like chicken need to be fully cooked to eat safely. Below are the minimum required temperatures for other types of meats.

* Poultry and other leftovers – 165°F or 74°C

* Beef – 145°F or 63°C

* Ground beef – 160°F or 71°C

* Pork – 150°F or 66°C

HOW TO USE A MEAT THERMOMETER

To check the temperature of a particular meat, insert the thermometer into the thickest section of the meat and get as close as possible to the center of it. You also want to check the temperature in multiple areas to make sure it is not being affected by a particular heated area of the meat. Do not get the thermometer close to the heat source or the reading won't be accurate. Do this as safely as possible, and when in doubt, always ask an adult for help.

DIFFERENT TYPES OF SUGARS, FLOURS, AND BUTTERS

When cooking, you will encounter different types of sugars, flours, and butters. In this section, we will cover the basic types of each category to give you a starting place to work with these ingredients. In most recipes, you will work with at least one of these, so it's an essential bit of knowledge to add to your cooking arsenal. Let's begin!

SUGARS

There are three main types of sugars: white, brown, and liquid sugars. In this book, we will mostly use a type of white sugar called granulated sugar, which is the most basic kind and the sugar that you will usually find in your home pantry. When a recipe calls for just "sugar" it always means granulated sugar, unless another type is specified. Here is a list of white sugars:

* White or granulated sugar
* Confectioners' or powdered sugar
* Fruit sugar
* Baker's special sugar
* Superfine sugar
* Coarse sugar
* Sanding sugar

Brown sugars are typically recommended when cooking foods with richer flavors, such as gingerbread, spice cakes, or BBQ sauces. Light brown sugars may be recommended for sweet sauces or marinades. If a recipe doesn't specify which type of brown sugar to use, you can use light brown sugar. Here is a list of brown sugars:

* Light and dark brown sugars
* Turbinado sugar
* Muscovado sugar
* Free-flowing brown sugar

The last type of sugar is liquid sugar. This type of sugar is ready to use and is often the go-to for coffee shops. Simple syrups are a form of liquid sugar, made with a 1:1 ratio of water and sugar, and is used to flavor drinks like dirty sodas. Here are the two main types of liquid sugars:

- ✸ Liquid sugar
- ✸ Invert sugar

FLOURS

The most common type of flour that you will find in most pantries and that will be used in this book is all-purpose flour. This type of flour is best used for making cookies, bread, waffles, pancakes, biscuits, and pizza dough. Another type of flour that you might find in your pantry is whole wheat flour. This flour is denser than all-purpose flour. It is also great for making cookies, bread, waffles, pizza dough, pasta, and scones. Other types of flours include:

- ✸ White whole wheat flour
- ✸ Pastry flour
- ✸ Cake flour
- ✸ Bread flour
- ✸ Self-rising flour
- ✸ Vital wheat gluten flour
- ✸ Gluten-free flour
- ✸ Sprouted flour
- ✸ Bleached flour

BUTTERS

There are more than eighteen kinds of butters that you can use in recipes. Here we will only touch on the main three types. First, we will start with sweet cream butter—this is the butter that most of us know about and use in our kitchen and is made by churning fresh cream. This type of butter is best used unsalted but can also be used salted. It is best for sautéing, baking, buttering toast, and glazing vegetables.

The second type of butter is cultured butter. This kind of butter is fermented longer than sweet cream butter and is treated with culture the way yogurt is. It can be either salted or unsalted and is best used for making biscuits, pancakes, shortbreads, and pound cakes.

The last type of butter we will cover here is European-style butter. This butter is churned longer than American-style butter and is very lightly cultured. It can be used to spread on toast or anything baking related.

No matter what type of butter you use, you can't really go wrong.

HOW TO MEASURE

One of the most essential parts of cooking is having accurate measurements. Dry and liquid ingredients are measured differently.

To measure dry ingredients such as flour, rice, or sugar, use small metal or plastic cups with handles. Scoop up the amount that you need and remove any excess by sweeping the top with a spoon or butter knife. You will find that each set of cups comes in different sizes. Some standard measurements to keep in mind are:

- ¼ cup (57 g)
- ⅓ cup (76 g)
- ½ cup (113 g)
- 1 cup (240 g)

To measure liquid ingredients such as water, milk, or juice, use a liquid measuring cup. In order to get an accurate measurement, it's best to place the cup level on the counter and bend down to read the measurement. Find the point on the graduated scale that coincides with the bottom of the curved surface of the liquid to get the proper liquid measurement. This curved surface is called the meniscus. Some standard measurements that you will find in a liquid measuring cup are:

- ⅛ cup (60 ml)
- ¼ cup (30 ml)
- ⅓ cup (75 ml)
- ½ cup (120 ml)
- ¾ cup (180 ml)
- 1 cup (240 ml)

LIQUID CONVERSION TABLE

Here is a simple liquid conversion table to use when doing measurements.

½ fl oz	1 tablespoon	15 ml
¾ fl oz	1½ tablespoons	22 ml
1 fl oz	2 tablespoons	30 ml
2 fl oz	¼ cup	60 ml
3 fl oz	6 tablespoons	90 ml
4 fl oz	½ cup	120 ml
5 fl oz	10 tablespoons	150 ml
6 fl oz	¾ cup	180 ml
8 fl oz	1 cup	240 ml
16 fl oz	2 cups/1 pint	480 ml

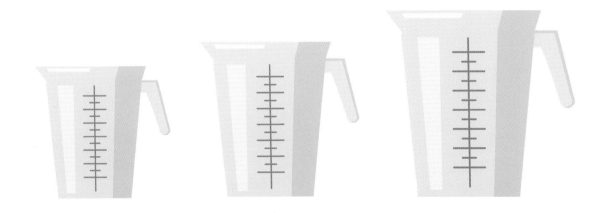

BREAKFAST

NO-BAKE HAZELNUT COCONUT BREAKFAST COOKIES

 Total Time: 1 hour and 10 minutes   Makes: 18 cookies

Ingredients

¼ cup (60 ml) milk
(2% or whole)

½ cup (1 stick or 115 g)
unsalted butter

¾ cup (150 g) sugar

½ cup (130 g) chocolate
hazelnut spread
(such as Nutella)

½ teaspoon vanilla extract

1 cup (80 g) old-fashioned
rolled oats, plus
6 tablespoons (30 g)
for topping (optional)

¾ cup (65 g) shredded
coconut flakes, for topping

Directions

1   In a small saucepan combine the milk, butter, and sugar and cook over medium heat. Mix until the butter melts, then bring to a boil. Let it boil for 1 minute.

2   Remove from the heat and stir in the chocolate hazelnut spread and vanilla. Once completely combined, add the 1 cup (80 g) oats and stir again.

3   Line a large baking sheet with parchment paper. Scoop balls of dough from the mixture, about 1 tablespoon (15 g) per cookie, and place a couple of inches (5 cm) apart on the prepared baking sheet.

4   Top with the shredded coconut flakes and remaining 6 tablespoons (30 g) rolled oats, if desired.

5   Refrigerate the cookies for at least 45 minutes until set before eating them.

 TIP: You can replace the chocolate hazelnut spread with peanut butter!

CINNAMON CRUNCH FRENCH TOAST

 Total Time: 20 minutes

 Makes: 4 slices

Ingredients

2 eggs

½ cup (120 ml) milk
(2% or whole)

½ teaspoon vanilla extract

¼ teaspoon ground cinnamon

4 slices thick bread

2 cups (82 g) Cinnamon Toast
Crunch cereal

2 tablespoons (28 g)
unsalted butter

Whipped cream, for topping

Directions

1   In a medium bowl, whisk together the eggs, milk, vanilla, and cinnamon. Working with one slice at a time, dip each slice of bread into the mixture until it is fully soaked, about 30 seconds.

2   In a separate bowl, add the cereal and crush with your hands. Transfer the soaked bread to the bowl with the cereal and press the bread into the cereal to coat.

3   In a large skillet over medium-low heat, melt the butter. Place the French toast in the skillet and cook for 3 minutes per side. Repeat with the remaining bread slices.

4   Transfer the French toasts to a plate. Top with whipped cream and serve.

 TIP: You can replace the Cinnamon Toast Crunch with any other of your favorite cereals!

FRENCH TOAST MADNESS

French toast is one of those breakfast items that you can be creative with in the kitchen. So, where did this amazing dish come from? French toast is said to have originated from a Roman Empire recipe known as *pan dulcis*. Here are two variations of French toast that you can try.

PICK YOUR FLAVOR

a. Mixed berries

b. S'mores

CREATE YOUR FILLING

Mixed Berries Sauce	S'mores Filling
2 cups (300 g) mixed berries, or blueberries, raspberries, and blackberries, plus more for topping 2 tablespoons (30 ml) lemon juice ⅓ cup (65 g) sugar	4 graham crackers 2 tablespoons (30 g) chocolate hazelnut butter (such as Nutella) 2 tablespoons (25 g) marshmallow creme (such as Fluff) 6 large marshmallows, halved, or 6 mini marshmallows, for topping Chocolate syrup, for additional topping

MAKE THE FRENCH TOAST

2 eggs

½ teaspoon vanilla extract

¼ teaspoon ground cinnamon

4 slices thick bread

2 tablespoons (28 g) unsalted butter

Maple syrup, for topping (optional)

Mixed Berries French Toast

1. In a medium or large bowl, whisk the eggs, vanilla, and cinnamon.
2. Toast your bread in a toaster or toaster oven on low for 1 to 2 minutes, just enough for the bread to dry out.
3. Dunk the bread slices into the egg mixture.
4. In a medium skillet over medium-low heat, melt the butter and cook the bread for 2 to 3 minutes, flipping slices on each side to cook.
5. Remove the cooked slices from the pan, place them on a plate, and set aside.
6. In a medium pan over low heat, combine the mixed berries, leaving a few out for topping (about 12), lemon juice, and sugar until a thick sauce is formed.
7. Add the berry mixture on top and in between your cooked bread slices, then stack the slices together.
8. Top with the reserved mixed berries and maple syrup, if desired.

S'mores French Toast

1. In a medium or large bowl, whisk the eggs, vanilla, and cinnamon.
2. Toast your bread in a toaster or toaster oven on low for 1 to 2 minutes, just enough for the bread to dry out.
3. Crush the graham crackers into crumbs either with your hands or in a blender. Place the crumbs in a separate medium bowl.
4. Dunk the bread in the egg mixture, then into the crumbs, coating the bread slices evenly.
5. In a medium skillet over medium-low heat, melt the butter and cook the bread for 2 to 3 minutes, flipping the slices on each side to cook.
6. On two slices, add the chocolate hazelnut spread; on the other two slices, add the marshmallow creme. Press one of each slice together as if you were making a sandwich and cook for an additional 30 seconds.
7. Remove the French toast from the pan, place on a plate, and top with the marshmallows, chocolate syrup, and maple syrup, if desired.

BACON, EGG & CHEESE BISCUIT BOMBS

 Total Time: 47 minutes   Makes: 10 biscuits

Ingredients

4 slices bacon

1 tablespoon (14 g) unsalted butter

3 eggs, divided

Pinch of black pepper

1 (10-ounce or 286-g) can refrigerated biscuits

¼ cup (56 g) grated cheddar cheese

1 tablespoon (15 ml) filtered water

Nonstick cooking spray

Directions

1 In a medium skillet over medium heat, cook the bacon, turning occasionally, until crisp, about 6 minutes. Remove from the pan and pat with a paper towel to remove grease.

2 Wipe the skillet with a small paper towel and add the butter. Once the butter has melted, add 2 of the eggs and a pinch of pepper. Scramble for about 2 minutes, ensuring the eggs are still moist, then remove.

3 Separate the biscuit dough into 5 biscuits and divide each biscuit into 2 layers. Add 1 tablespoon (15 g) of the egg mixture on the center of each round. Top with pieces of bacon and a sprinkling of the cheese. Gently fold the edges up and over the filling, pinching to seal.

4 In a small bowl, beat the remaining egg and the water. Brush the biscuits on all sides with the egg wash.

5 Place biscuits in an air fryer and cook at 325°F (165°C) for 8 minutes on one side. Flip over and cook for an additional 5 minutes. If using an oven, spray a 9 x 13-inch (23 x 33 cm) baking pan with nonstick cooking spray and preheat the oven at 325°F (165°C). Bake for 15 minutes.

6 Let cool and serve.

 TIP: You can swap the cheddar cheese with your favorite type of cheese to personalize it!

SAUSAGE BAGEL CASSEROLE

 Total Time: 1 hour   Makes: 6 servings

Ingredients

Nonstick cooking spray

3 (3-ounce or 85-g) everything bagels

4 large eggs

1¼ cups (300 ml) half-and-half

½ teaspoon kosher salt

¼ teaspoon black pepper

¾ teaspoon vegetable oil

8 ounces (227 g) breakfast sausage

½ cup (90 g) diced red bell pepper

½ cup (90 g) diced yellow onion

1 tablespoon (4 g) chopped fresh parsley

1½ cups (180 g) grated sharp cheddar cheese

Directions

1 Preheat the oven to 350°F (175°C). Spray a 9 x 13-inch (23 x 33 cm) casserole dish with nonstick cooking spray and set aside.

2 Cut each bagel into about 1-inch (2.5 cm) pieces.

3 In a medium mixing bowl, whisk together the eggs, half-and-half, salt, and black pepper until smooth.

4 Add the cut bagels to the egg mixture and use a large spoon to toss to coat the bagels with the liquid. Set aside so the bread can soak.

5 Heat the oil in a medium skillet over medium-high heat for about 1 minute. Add the breakfast sausage to the pan. Once it begins to brown, use a spatula to break up the sausage into small chunks until cooked through, about 5 minutes.

6 Add the diced bell pepper and onion. Stir and cook for 4 minutes.

7 Remove the mixture from the pan and let cool for 5 minutes.

8 Once the sausage has cooled, add it to the bagel and egg mixture. Add the parsley and cheddar cheese and combine well.

9 Pour the mixture into the prepared casserole dish and cover with aluminum foil.

10 Bake for 20 minutes, remove the foil, and bake for an additional 25 minutes. Serve warm.

A HOLEY HISTORY

Bagels are a very popular breakfast ingredient in the United States. While there is a lot of debate about who makes the best bagels, most New Yorkers will tell you that nobody beats their bagels. (Montreal may disagree . . .) But what is a bagel exactly and where does it come from?

In simpler terms, a bagel is a round bread with a hole in the middle. There are various flavors of bagels, such as plain, everything, cinnamon raisin, onion, garlic, poppy seed, and more. They can be enjoyed with a variety of spreads from cream cheese to butter to flavored jellies.

While the origin of the bagel is not really known, there are many theories that lead back to Poland. One theory suggests that the bagel dates as far back as the fourteenth century and appeared during the German migration to Poland. It is said to originate from a bread called *obwarzanek*, which means "to parboil" and refers to a cooking technique of boiling dough before baking. Although today the obwarzanek would be considered a different type of bread than the bagel, some believe the obwarzanek may have something to do with its origins.

Another theory suggests that the bagel originated in Austria in the seventeenth century by a Viennese baker. It is theorized that the baker created the bagel after the Battle of Vienna in 1683 to pay tribute to the Polish king, John III Sobieski.

It is said that the bagel came to the United States in the nineteenth century with the arrival of Jewish immigrants from Poland to New York. They sold the bagels in the streets of New York on the Lower East Side of Manhattan. This is the origin of the popular and iconic New York–style bagel. Although the bagel came to New York in the nineteenth century, it didn't gain popularity in the United States until the 1970s.

WHAT MAKES A NEW YORK–STYLE BAGEL DIFFERENT?

Many people ask themselves what makes the New York–style bagel different than other bagels. Well, the difference is said to come from New York City water, which contains low concentrations of magnesium and calcium and high levels of sediment. But while the water does make a difference, the real distinction comes from an additional step in the cooking process, which involves submerging the dough in boiling water for a few minutes before baking.

BERRY FROSTED PARFAIT

 Total Time: 10 minutes   Makes: 1 parfait

Ingredients

1 cup (240 ml) yogurt

2 tablespoons Frosted Flakes

½ cup (74 g) blueberries

½ cup (72 g) strawberries

Directions

1 In a small glass cup, pour half of the yogurt, half of the Frosted Flakes, half of the blueberries, and half of the strawberries.

2 Repeat step 1 with a second layer of yogurt, Frosted Flakes, and berries.

3 Serve and eat immediately.

FUN FACT

The oldest record of yogurt being eaten was in 6000 BCE in Central Asia!

CONFETTI WAFFLES

 Total Time: 25 minutes   Makes: 6 waffles

Ingredients

2 cups (240 g)
all-purpose flour

½ cup (100 g) sugar

2 teaspoons
baking powder

½ teaspoon salt

2 eggs

1 cup (240 ml) milk
(2% or whole)

⅓ cup (80 ml) vegetable oil

2 teaspoons vanilla extract

½ cup (75 g) rainbow
sprinkles, plus more for
topping (optional)

Nonstick cooking spray

Whipped cream, for topping
(optional)

Directions

1   Preheat a waffle iron.

2   In a large bowl, whisk together the flour, sugar, baking
    powder, and salt. Add the eggs, milk, oil, and vanilla
    and stir to make a smooth batter. Stir in the sprinkles.

3   Spray nonstick cooking spray onto the waffle iron.
    Spoon the batter into the waffle iron and close the lid.
    Cook for about 4 minutes, until golden brown.

4   Top with whipped cream and extra sprinkles!

TEST YOUR BREAKFAST KNOWLEDGE!

Have fun answering some cool questions about the healthiest meal of the day and add the answers to your cooking arsenal.

1. **Which meal is often referred to as the most important meal of the day?**

    a. Breakfast

    b. Lunch

    c. Dinner

    d. Dessert

2. **What is the healthiest breakfast you can have?**

    a. Eggs and spinach

    b. Toast and avocado

    c. Oatmeal and fruits

    d. All of the above

3. **People who regularly eat breakfast are able to focus better throughout the day and have a greater boost of energy. Is this statement true or false?**

    a. True

    b. False

4. **The world's first breakfast cereal was created on what date?**

    a. 1852

    b. 1863

    c. 1922

    d. 1902

5. **National Hot Breakfast Month is celebrated in which month?**

    a. January

    b. February

    c. March

    d. April

6. **Which country has the highest consumption of eggs?**

   a. United States
   b. Turkey
   c. Japan
   d. China

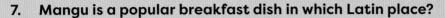

7. **Mangu is a popular breakfast dish in which Latin place?**

   a. Puerto Rico
   b. Cuba
   c. Dominican Republic
   d. Mexico

8. **Who made the very first pancakes in the first century CE?**

   a. Romans
   b. Greeks
   c. Egyptians
   d. Italians

9. **Which of the following is a national breakfast holiday?**

   a. National Egg Day
   b. National Pancake Day
   c. National Cereal Day
   d. All of the above

10. **What is the most popular breakfast item in the United States?**

    a. Bacon
    b. Sausage
    c. Eggs
    d. Pancakes

Answer key: 1. a, 2. d, 3. a, 4. b, 5. b, 6. c, 7. c, 8. a, 9. d, 10. c

AVOCADO TOAST WITH CREAMY SCRAMBLED EGGS

 Total Time: 25 minutes   Makes: 1 serving

Ingredients

1½ teaspoons (7.5 ml) olive oil

½ teaspoon lemon juice

2 pinches of salt and black pepper, divided

½ ripe avocado

1 slice bread

Nonstick cooking spray

1 egg

Directions

1   In a small bowl, combine the olive oil, lemon juice, and 1 pinch each of salt and pepper.

2   Scoop out the avocado flesh with a spoon and add it to the bowl. Use a fork to smash it until smooth.

3   Toast the bread in a toaster until golden on both sides, 1 to 2 minutes. Spread the avocado mixture on the toast.

4   Spray a small frying pan with nonstick cooking spray, then place over medium-low heat. When hot, after about 1 minute, crack the egg into the pan. Stir the egg with a spatula until it has combined and clumped together, about 2 minutes.

5   Sprinkle with the remaining pinch each of salt and pepper. Remove from the heat and place the egg on top of the avocado toast.

 TIP: Everything bagel seasoning pairs really well with this recipe combination as the perfect finish.

RAINBOW FRUIT SALAD

 Total Time: 15 minutes   Makes: 3 servings

Ingredients

1 cup (150 g) raspberries

1 cup (150 g) sliced strawberries

6 small mandarins, peeled and separated

1 cup (210 g) pineapple chunks

2 kiwis, peeled and sliced

1 cup (150 g) blueberries

Directions

On a large platter, assemble the fruit in a rainbow pattern. Start with raspberries, then proceed with strawberries, mandarins, pineapple, kiwi, and finish with blueberries.

 TIP: Fruit salad is the perfect side dish to go with any of the breakfast recipes in this book!

HOW TO PROPERLY SLICE A PINEAPPLE

1 Place the pineapple on a cutting board on its side. Place one hand on the handle of the knife and your other hand on the pineapple to steady it. Cut off the spiky top, then cut off the bottom of the pineapple.

2 Hold the pineapple upright and cut off the rind by slicing downward about ¼ inch (6 mm) into the rind. Be sure to use your non-cutting hand to steady the fruit as you slice.

3 Use a paring knife to remove any dark spots or patches. Then find the core (it's the dark yellow circle that is in the center), move your knife to the outer edge of it, and slice down from top to bottom, keeping the fruit upright as you do this.

4 Turn the pineapple about a quarter turn and slice down from top to bottom again. Repeat this until you have a couple of larger slices. Once done, cut horizontally through each large slice and then straight across to create smaller chunks.

* Cutting a pineapple can be difficult, so please ask an adult to help you with cutting, especially if this is your first time.

OVERNIGHT MINI TRES LECHES CINNAMON ROLLS

 Total Time: 9 hours and 20 minutes   Makes: 12 servings

Ingredients

Nonstick cooking spray

1 (17.5-ounce or 496-g) can refrigerated cinnamon rolls with icing (such as Pillsbury)

¾ cup (180 ml) canned sweetened condensed milk

¾ cup (180 ml) evaporated milk

½ cup (120 ml) whole milk

1 teaspoon vanilla extract

1½ cups (360 ml) whipped topping (such as Cool Whip), for topping (optional)

⅛ teaspoon ground cinnamon, for topping (optional)

12 strawberries, sliced, for serving

Directions

1 Preheat the oven to 350°F (175°C). Spray a baking sheet with nonstick cooking spray and set aside.

2 On a large cutting board, unroll the cinnamon roll and cut into equal-size strips, each 5 inches (12.5 cm) long.

3 Reroll each of the smaller strips in the cinnamon roll shape and place on the prepared baking sheet.

4 Bake for 12 to 15 minutes, or until golden.

5 Let the rolls cool completely, for 25 minutes, then place 8 of them in a 5 x 5-inch (13 x 13 cm) glass baking dish in a single layer.

6 In a medium bowl, mix the condensed milk, evaporated milk, whole milk, and vanilla extract until well combined. Pour half (1 cup or 240 ml) of the mixture evenly over the single layer of mini cinnamon rolls.

7 Using a butter knife, poke holes in the cinnamon rolls in the dish, about 4 holes per roll. Then, place the remaining mini rolls into the baking dish to cover the first layer.

8 Pour the remaining milk mixture on top, poking more holes into the cinnamon rolls, just enough for the mixture to soak into the rolls.

9 Cover the rolls with a plastic wrap or aluminum foil and refrigerate overnight or 8 hours, until most of the liquid has been absorbed into the cinnamon rolls.

10 To serve, remove the packaged icing from the refrigerator and spread over the soaked cinnamon roll mixture. Or if preferred, top with a whipped topping instead.

11 Sprinkle with cinnamon, if desired, and serve with sliced strawberries.

CHOCOLATE CHIP PROTEIN PANCAKE MUFFINS

 Total Time: 23 minutes   Makes: 6 muffins

Ingredients

Nonstick cooking spray (optional)

1 cup (120 g) pancake and waffle mix

¾ cup (180 ml) Greek yogurt

⅓ cup (80 ml) milk (2% or whole)

½ cup (90 g) chocolate chips, divided

Directions

1   Preheat the oven to 350°F (175°C). Line 6 cups of a regular-size muffin pan with liners or coat the muffin cups with nonstick cooking spray.

2   In a small bowl, combine the pancake mix, yogurt, and milk. Mix until smooth and then add ¼ cup (45 g) of the chocolate chips.

3   Scoop the mixture equally into the prepared muffin cups.

4   Top with the remaining ¼ cup (45 g) chocolate chips and bake for 15 minutes or until a toothpick inserted into the center of a muffin comes out clean.

5   Let cool for 5 minutes before enjoying.

 TIP: You can add ½ cup (74 g) of your favorite berries to the mixture to personalize to your liking!

FUN FACT

Four US states have adopted their own muffin flavors. New York has adopted apple muffins, Minnesota and Washington have adopted blueberry muffins, and Massachusetts has adopted corn muffins.

LUNCH

CHICKEN, RANCH & CHEESE ROLL-UPS

 Total Time: 1 hour and 15 minutes Makes: 12 roll-ups

Ingredients

1 cup (225 g) cream cheese, at room temperature

1 teaspoon dry ranch seasoning

1 cup (120 g) shredded cheddar cheese

4 large flour tortillas

6 slices deli chicken

Directions

1 In a small bowl, add the cream cheese and ranch seasoning and stir until combined. Add the cheddar cheese and stir together.

2 Lay out the tortillas and add one-quarter of the mixture to each, gently spreading it all over, right to the edges.

3 Cut the chicken into small pieces and layer one-quarter of the chicken on each tortilla.

4 Starting at one end, roll each tortilla until you get to the other side. Refrigerate for 1 hour.

5 Cut the ends off of each tortilla roll and discard, then cut each tortilla into 3 pieces and serve.

FUN FACT
Ranch dressing was created by a plumber named Steve Henson in the 1950s!

PEPPERONI PIZZA EMPANADAS

 Total Time: 25 minutes   Makes: 10 empanadas

Ingredients

½ cup (120 ml) marinara sauce, plus more for dipping

¾ cup (83 g) shredded mozzarella cheese

1 cup (145 g) mini pepperoni

10 pieces ready-made empanada dough (such as Goya)

Nonstick cooking spray

Directions

1   Place 1 teaspoon of marinara sauce, 1 tablespoon of cheese, and 8 to 10 pieces of pepperoni in the center of each disc of empanada dough.

2   Carefully fold each dough disc in half and use a fork to press firmly around the edges to seal.

3   Preheat the oven to 350°F (175°F) then add nonstick cooking spray and air-fry in batches for 8 to 10 minutes, making sure to turn them halfway through the cooking time, until golden.

4   Serve warm with marinara sauce for dipping.

   TIP: Change the fillings to your favorite pizza toppings.

FUN FACT

Empanadas are considered part of traditional Latin cuisine, and they have a variety of names, including empanadilla, empanadita, pastel, pastelillo, pastelito, and chamuco. Many Latin countries and islands have variations of this dish, and they can be filled with a variety of ingredients, including meats, cheeses, fruits, and vegetables. See page 60 for more empanada ideas!

BETTER THAN ABUELITA'S EMPANADAS

Empanadas are stuffed, baked, or fried pastries that are shaped like a half-moon. Although there are many variations of empanadas all over the world, today they are often associated with Latin cuisine. Empanadas can be savory or sweet and can have a variety of fillings. Have some fun making your very own empanadas.

PICK YOUR DOUGH

a. Use ready-made empanada dough (such as Goya)

b. Make fresh dough or masa

·············· Making Fresh Dough ··············

This recipe makes 16 empanadas, but you can double it if you are serving more people.

2 cups (240 g) all-purpose flour, plus more for dusting

½ teaspoon salt

¼ cup (½ stick or 55 g) unsalted butter, melted

2 egg yolks

½ cup (120 ml) water

1. In a large bowl, combine the flour and salt. Add the butter, egg yolks, and water and combine until a dough begins to form.

2. Transfer the dough to a flat surface lightly dusted with flour.

3. Knead the dough until it begins to come together. If the dough is too wet or sticky, add 1 tablespoon (10 g) of flour at a time until the dough no longer sticks to your hands.

4. Cover the dough with plastic wrap or a towel and refrigerate for 30 minutes.

5. Divide the dough into quarters and then each quarter into quarters for 16 pieces total. Roll each piece into a ball. On a flour-dusted surface, flatten the balls into a circle to add the fillings. Brush some egg wash (mixture of 1 egg and 1 tablespoon of water) on the top of your closed empanadas to give them a nice golden color.

PICK YOUR FILLINGS

- Cheese
- Beef
- Shrimp

- Chicken
- Guava
- Pork

- Crab
- Ham
- Veggies

- Black beans
- Pepperoni
- Turkey

PREPARE THE EMPANADAS

1. Once you have your chosen dough, you can begin to fill it with your favorite toppings. Make sure that any toppings that require you to cook beforehand (e.g., meat, seafood, or some veggies) are fully cooked before adding them in.

2. Fill up your empanada with the toppings of your choice. Be careful not to overfill your empanada or it will not close properly; 1 or 2 tablespoons of toppings should do it.

3. Carefully fold each dough disc in half and use a fork to seal the edge on both sides. If you notice that your empanada is breaking, then you may have overfilled it.

4. Bake or fry your empanada until golden brown on both sides. The timing will depend on the toppings you include and whether or not you've decided to bake or fry. Baking may take longer. Serve warm.

TERIYAKI CHICKEN LETTUCE WRAPS

 Total Time: 20 minutes   Makes: 4 wraps

Ingredients

1 cup (150 g) shredded
rotisserie chicken

¼ cup (40 g) chopped
red onion

¼ cup (27 g) shredded carrots

¼ cup (4 g) chopped
fresh cilantro

½ cup (120 ml) teriyaki sauce

4 leaves butter lettuce

1 lime

Directions

1 In a large mixing bowl, toss the chicken, onion, carrots, cilantro, and teriyaki sauce until coated.

2 Divide the chicken mixture equally among the lettuce leaves, using each leaf like a cup.

3 Slice the lime in half and squeeze lime juice over each of the cups. Serve immediately.

FUN FACT

Lettuce with darker colors contains more vitamins and minerals than lettuce with lighter colors.

CUBAN HAM & CHEESE SLIDERS

 Total Time: 30 minutes   Makes: 6 sliders

Ingredients

6 sweet dinner rolls (such as King's Hawaiian Original Hawaiian Sweet Rolls)

⅓ cup (70 g) mayonnaise

6 slices Swiss cheese

6 to 12 slices deli honey ham

1½ teaspoons poppy seeds

1½ tablespoons (22 ml) Dijon mustard

¼ cup (½ stick or 55 g) unsalted butter, melted

1½ teaspoons onion powder

¼ teaspoon Worcestershire sauce

Directions

1 Preheat the oven to 350°F (175°C).

2 Cut each roll in half and spread the mayonnaise on one half of each of the rolls.

3 Cut the Swiss cheese slices into fourths. Place 1 or 2 slices of ham and 1 slice of Swiss cheese on the bottom half of each roll. Place the top halves of the rolls on top and bunch the rolls closely together in a 10 x 15-inch (25 x 38 cm) baking dish.

4 In a medium bowl, whisk together the poppy seeds, Dijon mustard, melted butter, onion powder, and Worcestershire sauce. Pour the mixture over the rolls, just covering the top of them. Cover with foil and let sit for 10 minutes.

5 Bake for 10 minutes, or until the cheese is melted. Uncover and bake for an additional 2 minutes, or until the tops of the rolls are slightly browned and crisp. Serve warm.

 TIP: Add thinly sliced pickles for a more authentic Cuban taste.

THE HISTORY BEHIND CUBAN CUISINE

Cuban sliders are just the tip of the iceberg when it comes to Cuban cuisine. As the first island to be colonized and the last to gain its freedom from Spanish rule, Cuban food is greatly influenced by the Spanish as well as by the Indigenous Tainos and African and Caribbean cuisines.

During the colonial era, Havana was a major trading port, and as many Spanish people began to emigrate there, they brought with them their own cattle, pigs, and spices. Many colonizers were from southern Spain, which is why a lot of Cuban food is influenced by Andalusia. Many other food ingredients, including *malanga* (taro) and *tostones* (fried plantains), were also introduced once African slaves were brought to Cuba. This also led to African-influenced Cuban dishes such as *fufú*.

The Cuban revolution and the breakdown of US relations in the 1960s greatly impacted Cuban food. The rise of Fidel Castro led to many people leaving the island, including chefs and restaurant owners, while tense relations with the US and other countries greatly impacted their access to food supplies. Trading imports that were once plentiful were no longer available, which meant that the Cuban government had to figure out other ways to import goods into Cuba.

Once the Cuban government strengthened their ties to the Soviet Union, they were introduced to new foods such as pizza, yogurt, and wheat. All of this impacted the way Cubans had to think about and prepare their food. In Cuba, you will not find any American influence on their food. However, in Cuban immigrant communities that settled in the US, it is quite common to see this influence in their food.

Some of Cuba's staple foods include malanga, yuca, plantains, and seafood. While seafood is a popular dish, it is more common to see Cubans eating pork or chicken. Rice also became a major staple in Cuban cuisine over time as a side dish to other main dishes. Some of their most popular dishes are *ropa vieja* (which translates to "old clothes," but is a dish made of flank steak and veggies), *moros y cristianos* (mixed black beans and rice), and *lechon asado* (roasted pork).

Cuban food often consists of natural ingredients that grow in their tropical climate. The spices that are most common in Cuban cuisine include onion, garlic, bay leaves, coriander, black pepper, and cumin.

ONE-POT MAC 'N' CHEESE

 Total Time: 20 minutes   Makes: 6 servings

Ingredients

5 cups (1.2 L) whole milk

1 (30.35-ounce, or 850-g) box elbow macaroni

½ cup (1 stick or 115 g) unsalted butter

2 cups (240 g) shredded cheddar cheese

Salt and black pepper, to taste , plus more black pepper for topping (optional)

Directions

1 In a large pot over medium-high heat, gently heat the milk to a simmer.

2 Once simmering, add the macaroni and cook until the pasta is tender, about 8 minutes.

3 Once the noodles are cooked, turn off the heat and add the butter, cheddar, and salt and pepper to the pot. Stir the ingredients with the pasta until the cheese and butter melt into the milk to create a thick sauce.

4 Finish with a grinding of pepper, if preferred. Serve warm.

 TIP: Sprinkle with cooked bacon pieces to change it up!

SPINACH GRILLED CHEESE

 Total Time: 7 minutes   Makes: 2 sandwiches

Ingredients

2 cups (60 g) baby spinach

½ cup (60 g) shredded cheddar cheese

2 tablespoons (30 g) cream cheese

Pinch of salt

4 slices bread of choice

1 tablespoon (14 g) unsalted butter

Directions

1 Add the spinach, cheese, cream cheese, and salt to a food processor and blend until smooth.

2 Spread the spinach mixture on 2 slices of bread. You can add as much or as little as you want but the more you add the cheesier it will be.

3 In a medium skillet over medium heat, melt the butter. Add the prepared bread slices to the pan with the filling sides facing up.

4 Top each with the remaining bread slices and cook for 4 minutes. Flip over and cook for an additional 4 minutes, or until golden brown and the filling has melted. Remove from the heat and cut in half before serving.

FUN FACT

Because Americans tend to throw bread out once it is stale, bread is one of the most wasted food products in the US.

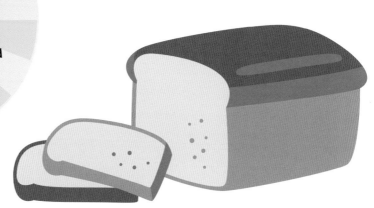

GETTING CHEESY

Most of us love cheese, and can't get enough of it. It's also in most savory dishes. Do you see any of your favorite cheeses on this list?

American: This is a great cheese to add to sandwiches and burgers.

Asiago: This Italian cheese can be melted in sandwiches, served with crackers, or added on top of dishes such as pizza or casseroles.

Brie: This French cheese is great for appetizers and is generally paired with bread, crackers, fruits, or nuts.

Cheddar: This versatile English cheese is used in most comfort foods and is one of the most popular cheeses in America.

Colby: This American cheese is not commonly used in cooking but is popular for snacking and topping sandwiches.

Feta: This versatile cheese originally from Greece is commonly used for appetizers and to garnish dishes such as pasta, potatoes, and salads.

Goat: This cheese originated in the Mediterranean and Middle East and is used in a variety of ways and can be spread on bagels and breads, crumbled over salads, or added to soups, pastas, and pizza.

Gouda: This cheese is an original of the Netherlands and another great melting cheese, often used in macaroni and cheese.

Grana Padano: This is one of the most popular cheeses in Italy and is great for grating over pasta or risotto.

Gruyère: This Swiss original is another great melting cheese that can be used in dishes like soufflés and fondue and be grated for topping salads and pastas.

Manchego: This cheese is traditionally served in Spanish tapas and paired with bread, ham, and olives.

Monterey Jack: This American cheese is also great for melting and most commonly used in quesadillas and burritos.

Mozzarella: This Italian cheese is most commonly used for topping pizza.

Parmesan: This is another Italian original that is most often used grated.

Pepper Jack: This American cheese has a spicy element and is also very versatile, often used in dishes like grilled sandwiches and quesadillas.

Provolone: Another Italian original, this cheese is also versatile and great for snacking or sandwiches.

Swiss: This American cheese has Swiss origins and can be used in sandwiches, burgers, pastas, pastries, and omelets. It has holes that are caused by the carbon dioxide that is released by the bacteria used in making it.

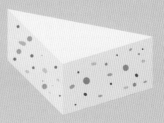

EASY TOMATO SOUP

 Total Time: 50 minutes   Makes: 2 cups (480 ml)

Ingredients

¼ cup (½ stick or 55 g) unsalted butter

½ large onion, cut into large wedges

1½ cups (360 ml) low-sodium vegetable or chicken stock or broth

1 (28-ounce, or 784-g) can whole, peeled, or crushed tomatoes

½ teaspoon salt

Directions

1 In a large saucepan over medium heat, melt the butter.

2 Add the onion, stock, tomatoes (with all the juices), and salt. Bring to a simmer and cook, uncovered, for about 40 minutes, stirring occasionally so the soup doesn't stick to the bottom of the pan.

3 Turn off the heat and let the soup cool for about 10 minutes.

4 Once cooled, carefully transfer the mixture to a blender and blend to your preferred texture.

 TIP: This soup recipe pairs nicely with the Spinach Grilled Cheese on page 70.

CRUNCHY BEEF QUESADILLAS

 Total Time: 18 minutes   Makes: 2 quesadillas

Ingredients

2 tablespoons (30 ml) vegetable oil

10 ounces (280 g) ground beef

1 (1-ounce or 28-g) packet taco seasoning

Salt and black pepper, to taste

2 large flour tortillas

1 cup (120 g) shredded Mexican cheese blend

1 (9-ounce or 252-g) bag nacho cheese chips (such as Doritos)

Directions

1 In a medium saucepan over medium heat, add the oil. Once hot, add the ground beef and cook for about 8 minutes.

2 Add the taco seasoning and salt and pepper to the beef and cook for another 5 minutes. Remove from the pan and set aside.

3 Lay the tortillas on a cutting board and spread the ground beef and cheese on ½ of each of the tortillas, then top with 4 to 6 nacho cheese chips.

4 Fold the tortillas over and cut into 3 triangle slices. Try to get these slices as even as you can, but they don't have to be perfect!

5 Place the tortillas in a large dry skillet and toast for 2 minutes on each side, or until the cheese has melted.

 TIP: Fillings for this quesadilla recipe are endless. You can add anything from tomatoes and lettuce to sour cream and beans.

BACON-WRAPPED HOT DOGS

 Total Time: 20 minutes

 Makes: 4 hot dogs

Ingredients

4 slices bacon
(pork, beef, or turkey)

4 hot dogs

Nonstick cooking spray

4 hot dog buns

Directions

1 Take 1 piece of bacon and wrap it tightly around each hot dog so the edges of the bacon touch but do not overlap. Secure the ends with a couple of toothpicks.

2 Preheat an air fryer to 400°F (200°C) for 5 minutes and spray the air fryer basket with nonstick cooking spray.

3 Add the bacon-wrapped hot dogs to the air fryer basket and cook for 8 minutes. Flip the hot dogs and cook for another 3 to 5 minutes, until the bacon is cooked to your preferred crispness.

4 Remove the hot dogs from the air fryer and let them cool for 1 to 2 minutes.

5 Remove the toothpicks and place the hot dogs into the buns.

 TIP: Top hot dogs with your favorite toppings, like ketchup, relish, mustard, and cheese!

FUN FACT

Hot dogs were one of the first foods eaten by Neil A. Armstrong and Edwin E. "Buzz" Aldrin Jr. on their monumental mission to outer space.

MASON-JAR FETA SALAD

 Total Time: 7 minutes   Makes: 2 servings

Ingredients

8 ribs celery, sliced into bite-size pieces

½ cup (75 g) grape tomatoes, sliced in half

½ cup (83 g) chickpeas

½ cup (60 g) crumbled feta cheese

⅓ cup (80 ml) dressing of choice

Directions

1 Divide the celery equally between two 32-ounce (946 ml) mason jars, followed by the chickpeas, tomatoes, and feta cheese.

2 Top off both jars with the dressing.

3 You can refrigerate the salad in the mason jars for up to 3 days.

 TIP: Make your own dressing by combining ⅓ cup (80 ml) olive oil, ⅓ cup (80 ml) vinegar, and salt and black pepper to taste and mixing well.

HOW TO CUT CELERY

1 Wash the celery ribs and pat them dry with a clean kitchen towel or paper towel.

2 Trim the ends of the celery to remove the parts that don't look as fresh.

3 Place one hand on your knife and the other holding on to the celery firmly. Be sure to have your hand safely away from your knife to keep from accidentally cutting yourself.

4 If you want smaller dices of celery, cut the stalks lengthwise (vertically) before you make your desired cuts.

5 Stack the trimmed celery stalks together and cut across at the desired thickness.

DINNER

RAINBOW FRIED RICE

 Makes: 6 servings

Ingredients

2 teaspoons vegetable oil

½ red bell pepper, diced small

1 medium carrot, peeled and diced small

½ cup (45 g) chopped red cabbage

3 cups (600 g) cooked rice or quinoa

¼ cup (55 g) frozen corn

¼ cup (55 g) frozen peas

¼ teaspoon garlic powder

3 tablespoons (45 ml) low-sodium soy sauce

Directions

1 In a large skillet over medium heat, add the oil and heat for 1 minute. Add the bell pepper, carrot, and cabbage and cook, stirring occasionally, until softened, about 3 minutes.

2 Add the rice, corn, peas, and garlic powder and stir to combine. Cook for about 2 minutes, then add the soy sauce and stir to combine.

 TIP: You can change the vegetables for any of your preference.

HOW TO COOK RICE

1 In a colander, add 2 cups (330 g) long-grain white rice and rinse under running water for 1 to 2 minutes. This step is optional if you prefer not to rinse your rice.

2 In a medium caldero or saucepan over high heat, add 2 cups (480 ml) water, ½ teaspoon salt, and 1 tablespoon (15 ml) oil and bring to a boil. Stir in the rice and let the water return to a simmer. Stir again, cover the pot, turn the heat down to low, and let cook for 15 minutes.

3 Uncover the rice and stir. Cover and let cook for another 10 minutes.

BLACK BEAN TACOS

 Total Time: 7 minutes　　 Makes: 6 tacos　　

Ingredients

1 (15.5-ounce or 439-g) can black beans

1 teaspoon vegetable oil

2 tablespoons (30 g) adobo paste

2 tablespoons (18 g) taco seasoning

½ cup (60 g) shredded cheddar cheese

½ cup (60 g) Mexican cheese blend

6 flour tortillas

Sour cream, for topping (optional)

Lime wedges, for topping (optional)

Chopped fresh cilantro, for topping (optional)

Directions

1 Drain and rinse the beans under running water.

2 In a medium pan over medium-high heat, add the oil and heat for about 1 minute. Add the adobo paste and taco seasoning and cook for about 30 seconds, then add the beans. Stir until well combined.

3 Sprinkle both cheeses over the beans. Turn off the heat, cover the pan, and let sit for 1 minute, or until the cheese melts.

4 Warm the tortillas by wrapping them in a paper towel and popping them in the microwave for 30 seconds.

5 Fill the tortillas with the black bean filling and top with sour cream, lime wedges, and chopped fresh cilantro, if desired.

FUN FACT

Black beans are a great source of folic acid, magnesium, potassium, and iron.

HERBAL MAGIC

Herbs are a great way to add flavor to dishes or to elevate a dish. Don't be afraid to experiment with them. Some things to consider as you are working with herbs:

- Wash and dry your herbs before using them. You can use a salad spinner for drying if you have one.

- Remove leaves from stems and discard the stems before chopping the leaves.

- When working with fresh herbs, wait until you are ready to use them before chopping; otherwise, they can become limp and dried out.

FRESH HERBS VS. DRIED HERBS

Dried herbs tend to be less expensive and have a more concentrated flavor than fresh herbs. Some herbs are better used fresh, such as cilantro, parsley, and basil, but generally, deciding to use one or the other depends on the dish you are making and the flavor that you are looking for. For the most part, dried herbs are better used for cooked dishes such as soups, while fresh herbs may be better served in uncooked dishes such as guacamole. Here are a few main herbs and their uses.

- **Basil:** This herb is most often used in Italian dishes such as pesto and sauces. Sweet and Genovese basil are the most common varieties and are great for pairing with tomato.

- **Chives:** This herb is best used as a garnish to enhance a dish. It can be used in soups, dips, eggs, potatoes, and seafood dishes. It also adds a garlic-like flavor to dishes.

- **Cilantro:** This herb is a staple in Latin, Mediterranean, and Asian cuisines. The stem has a wonderful flavor and is okay to cut with the leaves.

- **Dill:** This herb is typically used in European and Middle East cuisines. It is best with seafood, soups, salads, and sauces. This is usually the number one herb used for seasoning fish, and it also works paired with cucumber dishes.

- **Mint:** Mint adds a very peppery and cooling flavor to dishes. This herb is used in Middle Eastern and North African cuisines and adds fresh flavor to salads and drinks.

- **Oregano:** This herb is generally found dried over fresh and is typically used in Mexican and Mediterranean cuisines. You can use this herb in eggs, omelets, meat dishes, tomato dishes, and much more.

- **Parsley:** This is a common and versatile herb that is used in many recipes. It's most often used to add color and flavor at the end of cooking as a garnish.

- **Thyme:** This is a common herb in American and European cooking and is best paired with meat, chicken, fish, and potatoes. It also pairs well with oregano. Thyme works well cooked and in soups.

CHICKEN NUGGETS

 Total Time: 1 hour and 58 minutes   Makes: 24 nuggets

Ingredients

1 pound (454 g) boneless, skinless chicken breast

½ teaspoon Italian seasoning

½ teaspoon garlic powder

½ teaspoon paprika

1 teaspoon salt

½ teaspoon black pepper

1 egg

1¼ cups (145 g) panko bread crumbs

Nonstick cooking spray

BBQ SAUCE
(makes 1½ cups or 360 ml)

1 In a small saucepan over medium heat, combine ⅔ cup (165 ml) ketchup, ½ cup (120 ml) apple cider vinegar, ¼ cup (50 g) brown sugar, 2 teaspoons (8 g) smoked paprika, 1 teaspoon ground cumin, 1 teaspoon kosher salt, and 1 teaspoon pepper. Bring the mixture to a simmer and cook for 5 minutes.

2 Pour the sauce into a medium bowl. Let cool for 20 minutes before serving.

Directions

1 On a large cutting board, cut the chicken into cubes. Add the chicken cubes to a food processor and pulse to get a thick consistency with small chunks (not a ground meat texture). Transfer to a large bowl. Add the Italian seasoning, garlic powder, paprika, salt, and pepper and stir to combine.

2 Shape the chicken mixture into rounded 1½-inch (4 cm) squares or rectangles.

3 In a small bowl, crack the egg and beat until smooth. Spread the bread crumbs in a shallow bowl or plate.

4 Dip each nugget into the egg mixture and then dredge in the bread crumbs to thoroughly coat.

5 Place the nuggets on a baking sheet and freeze for 1 hour.

6 Preheat an air fryer at 350°F (175°C), then lightly spray the nuggets with nonstick cooking spray and place 6 to 8 nuggets at a time in the air fryer basket. Cook at 350°F (175°C) for 6 minutes. Turn the nuggets over and cook for another 6 minutes. If you prefer extra-crispy nuggets, cook for an additional 3 minutes. (If using an oven, preheat it to 400°F or 205°C and coat a 9 x 13-inch or 23 x 33-cm baking pan with nonstick cooking spray. Bake the chicken nuggets for 10 minutes, then flip them over and cook for another 10 minutes, or until they are browned.)

 TIP: Serve these nuggets with a side of BBQ sauce (see box on left), honey mustard, or ketchup.

STEAK & BROCCOLI

 Total Time: 25 minutes   Makes: 4 servings

Ingredients

3 tablespoons (30 g) cornstarch, divided

½ cup plus 2 tablespoons (150 ml) lukewarm water, divided

½ teaspoon garlic powder

1 pound (454 g) boneless round or charcoal chuck steak, cut into thin 3-inch-long (7.5 cm) strips

2 tablespoons (30 ml) vegetable oil, divided

1 small onion, cut into wedges

4 cups (280 g) broccoli florets

⅓ cup (80 ml) low-sodium soy sauce

2 tablespoons (25 g) brown sugar

1 teaspoon ground ginger

Toasted sesame seeds, for garnish (optional)

Directions

1 In a large bowl, combine 2 tablespoons (20 g) of the cornstarch, 2 tablespoons (30 ml) of the water, and the garlic powder. Stir until smooth, then add the steak and toss to coat.

2 In a large skillet or wok over medium-high heat, add 1 tablespoon (15 ml) of the oil and let it heat for 1 minute. Add the steak and stir-fry until it reaches your desired doneness. Transfer to a plate and set aside.

3 Add the remaining 1 tablespoon (15 ml) oil to the skillet, add the onion wedges, and cook and stir for 5 minutes, or until softened. Add the broccoli and cook and stir for 3 minutes, or until the broccoli is tender but still crisp.

4 In a small bowl, add the soy sauce, brown sugar, ginger, remaining 1 tablespoon (10 g) cornstarch, and remaining ½ cup (120 ml) water. Stir well to dissolve the cornstarch.

5 Add the beef back to the pan with the broccoli mixture and add the soy sauce mixture. Cook and stir for 2 minutes, making sure to coat everything with the sauce.

6 Garnish with toasted sesame seeds, if desired.

 TIP: You can serve this dish over rice (see page 83).

SUPER FOODS FOR SUPER KIDS

No matter what vegetables you decide to eat, your body will thank you. Vegetables have many benefits for your overall health. It's essential to eat a variety of vegetables daily so that you keep yourself healthy and strong.

GREEN VEGETABLES

Let's begin with leafy green vegetables. Leafy greens provide many benefits, including detoxifying the body, improving heart health, and boosting brain function. They are full of calcium, potassium, iron, antioxidants, folate, fiber, and vitamins A, B6, C, and K. Darker leafy vegetables such as kale and spinach are healthier than lighter-colored greens because they tend to carry more nutrients. Leafy vegetables include the following:

- Arugula
- Beet greens
- Bok choy
- Broccoli
- Cabbage
- Collard greens

- Kale
- Mustard greens
- Romain lettuce
- Spinach
- Swiss chard
- Watercress

RED AND ORANGE VEGETABLES

Similar to their green counterparts, red and orange vegetables also carry many benefits and can improve your overall health. Orange and red vegetables provide fiber, potassium, and vitamins A, C, and K. One of the many benefits of these colored veggies is reducing the risk of cancer. Some red and orange vegetables include:

- Carrots
- Pumpkins
- Red and orange bell peppers
- Sweet potatoes
- Winter squash

- Red cabbage
- Beets
- Red and orange tomatoes
- Orange cauliflower
- Yams

ONE-POT SPAGHETTI

 Total Time: 23 minutes   Makes: 6 servings

Ingredients

1 pound (454 g) ground beef

2½ cups (600 ml) beef broth

1 (24-ounce or 680-g) jar marinara sauce

1 (14.5-ounce or 411-g) can diced tomatoes with basil, garlic, and oregano, drained

1 teaspoon garlic powder

8 ounces (227 g) uncooked spaghetti

Grated Parmesan cheese, for serving

Directions

1 In a large skillet over medium heat, add the ground beef. Cook, breaking up the meat with a wooden spoon, until browned, about 10 minutes. Drain the grease into a bowl or cup covered in aluminum foil, keeping the meat in the skillet. Be sure not to drain the grease into the sink.

2 Add the broth, marinara sauce, diced tomatoes, and garlic powder. Bring the mixture to a boil, then stir in the spaghetti and cook, stirring frequently, for 15 minutes or until the pasta is tender and the sauce is thick.

3 Serve with grated Parmesan.

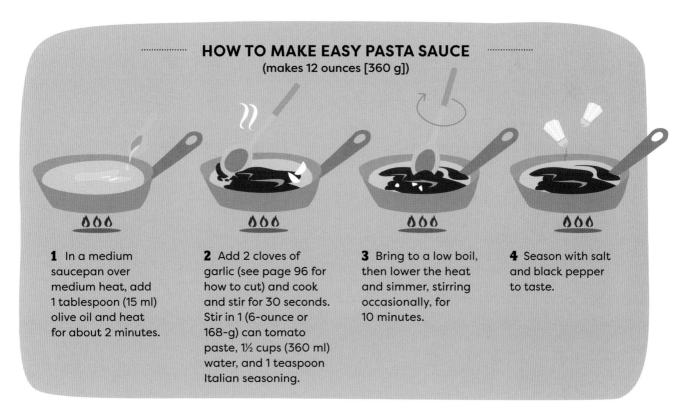

HOW TO MAKE EASY PASTA SAUCE
(makes 12 ounces [360 g])

1 In a medium saucepan over medium heat, add 1 tablespoon (15 ml) olive oil and heat for about 2 minutes.

2 Add 2 cloves of garlic (see page 96 for how to cut) and cook and stir for 30 seconds. Stir in 1 (6-ounce or 168-g) can tomato paste, 1½ cups (360 ml) water, and 1 teaspoon Italian seasoning.

3 Bring to a low boil, then lower the heat and simmer, stirring occasionally, for 10 minutes.

4 Season with salt and black pepper to taste.

CREAMY LEMON SPINACH RAVIOLI

 Total Time: 30 minutes   Makes: 4 servings

Ingredients

2 (18-ounce or 500-g) packages frozen spinach ricotta ravioli

2 teaspoons olive oil, divided

2 cloves garlic, cut in half

2 medium tomatoes, cut into ½-inch (13 mm) pieces

2 medium bell peppers, cut into ½-inch (13 mm) pieces

2 teaspoons bouillon powder

¼ cup (60 g) cream cheese

¼ cup (60 ml) sour cream

½ cup (60 g) grated Parmesan cheese, divided

2 tablespoons (28 g) unsalted butter

Zest and juice of 1 lemon

Salt and black pepper, to taste

Directions

1 Bring a large pot of water to a boil over high heat. Add the ravioli and cook, stirring occasionally, until al dente and floating to the top, 4 to 5 minutes. Reserve ½ cup (120 ml) of the cooking water and then drain the rest.

2 In a large saucepan, heat 1 teaspoon of the olive oil, then add the garlic, tomatoes, bell peppers, and bouillon and sauté for 2 minutes. Add the reserved cooking water, cream cheese, sour cream, ¼ cup (30 g) of the Parmesan cheese, and butter and whisk until creamy.

3 Add the lemon juice to taste. Season with salt and pepper.

4 Add the drained ravioli to the pan with the sauce and gently toss until thoroughly coated with the sauce.

5 Serve the ravioli with the sauce and top with the remaining ¼ cup (30 g) Parmesan and lemon zest to taste.

HOW TO CUT GARLIC, TOMATOES, AND BELL PEPPERS

Garlic: To release the cloves from your garlic bulb, use the bottom of a measuring cup to press down on the bulb. The papery skin will loosen, making the clove easier to peel. Peel the cloves carefully using your fingers (see also page 16). Once peeled, use a small knife to trim the edges of the clove and cut in half.

Tomatoes: To cut the tomatoes, place each tomato on a cutting board and place one hand on the handle of your knife and use the other to hold the tomato steady. Slice the tomato in half, then continue to cut into slices. Then, cut the slices into ½ inch pieces.

Bell peppers: To learn how to cut bell peppers, see page 19.

TEST YOUR PASTA KNOWLEDGE!

Most of us have eaten some version of pasta and love it! There are so many different types of pasta and they can be made in a variety of ways. Here are some common types of pastas and some fun questions to answer about pasta to sharpen your knowledge.

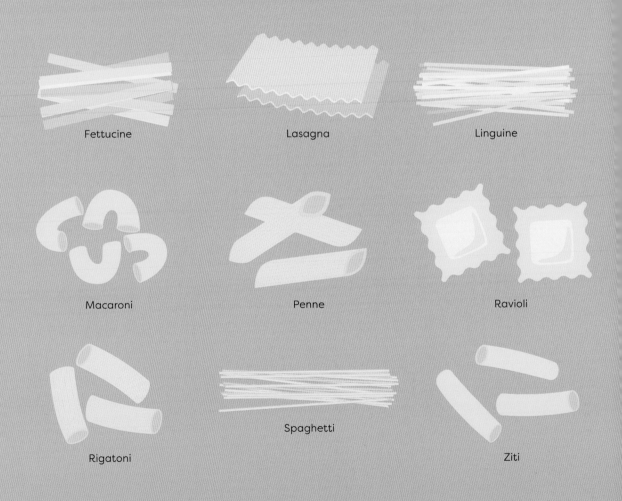

Fettucine

Lasagna

Linguine

Macaroni

Penne

Ravioli

Rigatoni

Spaghetti

Ziti

1. **There is evidence that suggests that Etruscans made pasta as early as what year?**

   a. 1000 BCE

   b. 400 BCE

   c. 500 BCE

   d. 2000 BCE

2. **In what month is World Pasta Day?**

   a. January

   b. April

   c. August

   d. October

3. **The most expensive spaghetti dish is sold in BiCE in New York; it costs $2,013 and is called what?**

   a. Lobster and Black Truffle Tagliolini

   b. Truffle Tagliolini Gold

   c. Finest Spaghetti

   d. Diamond Delicious Spaghetti

4. **Which pasta is in the form of small hollow tubes of different sizes?**

   a. Lasagna

   b. Ravioli

   c. Rigatoni

   d. Fettucine

5. **How many different types of pasta shapes are there today?**

   a. 100

   b. Over 600

   c. 50

   d. 300

Answer key: 1. b, 2. d, 3. a, 4. c, 5. b

CHEESY LOADED MASHED POTATOES

 Total Time: 35 minutes   Makes: 4 servings

Ingredients

1½ pounds (680 g) russet potatoes, peeled and cut into large dice

Pinch of salt, plus more to taste

2 slices bacon

¼ cup (½ stick or 55 g) unsalted butter, cut into pieces

1 cup (240 ml) sour cream

½ cup (60 g) shredded cheddar cheese

Black pepper, to taste

½ cup (24 g) chopped fresh chives, for garnish (optional)

Directions

1 Fill a large pot with water and bring to a boil over high heat. Add the potatoes and the pinch of salt, reduce the heat to medium-low, and simmer until tender, about 15 minutes. Drain the potatoes and return them to the pot.

2 In a medium skillet over medium-high heat, add the bacon and cook, turning occasionally, until crisp and browned, about 6 minutes. Transfer the bacon to a plate lined with paper towels to absorb the grease.

3 Add the butter to the potatoes and mash using a potato masher or a fork. Add the sour cream and continue to mash until well combined.

4 Crumble the bacon into the potato mixture and stir in the cheddar cheese. Season with salt and pepper.

5 Garnish with chives for extra flavor and color, if desired.

HOMEMADE PIZZA

 Total Time: 34 minutes   Makes: 6 servings

Ingredients

1¾ cups (220 g) all-purpose flour, plus more for dusting

2 teaspoons baking powder

1¼ cups (300 ml) plain Greek yogurt

Nonstick cooking spray

¾ cup (180 ml) pizza sauce

1 cup (120 g) shredded mozzarella cheese

Toppings of choice

Directions

1 In a large bowl, combine the flour, baking powder, and yogurt until well mixed (mix the dough until it stops sticking to your fingers). Shape the dough into a ball. Place the dough in a bowl and cover with plastic wrap. Set aside and let rest for 30 minutes.

2 Preheat the oven to 430°F (220°C). Line a large baking sheet or pizza pan with parchment paper and lightly oil the paper with nonstick cooking spray. Set aside.

3 Lightly dust a work surface with flour and roll out the dough with a rolling pin into a 10-inch (25 cm) circle.

4 Transfer the dough to the prepared baking sheet. Spread the pizza sauce on top, sprinkle with the mozzarella cheese, and add any toppings you want.

5 Bake for 15 to 17 minutes, until the cheese is melted and the crust is golden brown and crispy.

 TIP: You can season the pizza dough with Italian seasoning for added flavor.

MONTEREY JACK CHEESEBURGERS

 Total Time: 30 minutes   Makes: 2 cheeseburgers

Ingredients

10 ounces (280 g)
ground beef

Salt and black pepper,
to taste

Vegetable oil

½ cup (60 g) shredded
Monterey Jack cheese

½ tablespoon butter

2 burger buns

Directions

1   Line a cutting board with parchment paper and place the ground beef on top (to avoid cross-contamination). Divide the ground beef into two equal-size pieces and shape into patties. Season the patties on both sides with salt and pepper.

2   In a medium pan over medium-high heat, heat a drizzle of oil and add the patties to the pan. Cook almost to your desired doneness, 3 to 5 minutes per side.

3   Top each patty with the cheese. Cover the pan to melt the cheese and allow the patties to finish cooking, 1 to 2 minutes.

4   While the burgers are cooking, in a separate pan, melt the butter, then spread a small amount of butter on each bun half and place into the skillet on low-medium heat. Toast the bun halves until golden. Use a spatula to flip over the buns to toast on the other side.

5   Remove the patties from the pan and serve on the buns.

   TIP: Serve your burger with any of your favorite condiments, such as ketchup, mayonnaise, or pickles.

FUN FACT

Monterey Jack cheese originated with Franciscan friars in Monterey, California, in the eighteenth century. David Jacks was a businessman who sold the cheese as his own, hence the name Jack added to the cheese's name.

AIR FRYER ROASTED SWEET POTATO FRIES

 Total Time: 22 minutes   Makes: 2 servings

Ingredients

2 medium sweet potatoes

2 teaspoons olive oil

½ teaspoon salt

¼ teaspoon garlic powder

¼ teaspoon paprika

⅛ teaspoon black pepper

Nonstick cooking spray

Directions

1 Preheat an air fryer for 5 minutes at 380°F (195°C). While the air fryer is preheating, peel the sweet potatoes, then slice each potato into even ¼-inch-thick (6 mm) sticks. To soften the sweet potatoes for cutting, poke several holes into the skin with a fork then microwave for 1 to 2 minutes. Be sure to use an oven mitt to remove the potato from the microwave; it will be really hot! Ask an adult to help you with this.

2 In a large mixing bowl, add the sweet potato sticks, drizzle with the olive oil, and sprinkle with the salt, garlic powder, paprika, and pepper. Toss to thoroughly coat the sweet potato sticks.

3 Spray the air fryer with nonstick cooking spray. Then cook the fries in batches, depending on the size of your air fryer, for 6 minutes, then flip the fries over and cook for another 6 minutes, or until crispy. Serve immediately.

 TIP: Serve with your favorite dipping sauce.

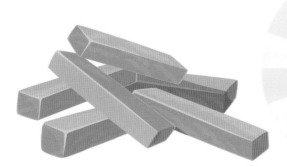

FUN FACT

Did you know that North Carolina's official vegetable is the sweet potato?

SNACKS

SWEET & SALTY TRAIL MIX

 Total Time: 1 hour   Makes: 5 cups (750 g)

Ingredients

Nonstick cooking spray

2 cups (454 g) corn chips
(such as Original Bugles)

2 cups (50 g) crispy rice
cereal squares

½ cup (22 g) small salted
pretzel twists

½ cup (65 g) pecan halves

¾ cup (150 g) firmly packed
brown sugar

½ cup (1 stick or 115 g)
unsalted butter

3 tablespoons (45 ml) light
corn syrup

½ teaspoon salt

1 teaspoon vanilla extract

½ teaspoon baking soda

1½ cups (280 g)
candy-coated chocolate
(such as M&M's)

Directions

1 Preheat the oven to 375°F (190°C). Spray a large
   roasting pan with nonstick cooking spray.

2 In a large bowl, add the corn chips, rice cereal, pretzels,
   and pecans and stir to combine. Spread over the
   prepared baking sheet.

3 In a medium saucepan over medium heat, combine
   the brown sugar, butter, corn syrup, and salt and cook,
   stirring occasionally, until the mixture comes to a full
   boil. Remove from the heat and stir in the vanilla and
   baking soda.

4 Pour the syrup mixture over the cereal mixture and toss
   to thoroughly coat.

5 Bake for 15 minutes, carefully stirring every 5 minutes.

6 Remove from the oven and spread the mixture onto
   a piece of wax paper to cool. Once cooled, stir in the
   candy-coated chocolates. Break into pieces to serve.

BANANA SUSHI

 Total Time: 5 minutes   Makes: 10 pieces

Ingredients

¼ cup (45 g) dark chocolate chips

2 bananas

3 tablespoons (15 g) Fruity Pebbles

Directions

1   In a microwave-safe bowl, melt the chocolate in the microwave in 30-second intervals, stirring after each interval, until it becomes smooth enough to dip the bananas into. Be careful not to overcook.

2   Peel the bananas, cut each into 5 pieces, then carefully dip them into the melted chocolate using a fork or stick.

3   Add the Fruity Pebbles to a medium bowl, then roll the dipped bananas in them to coat. Line them up to look like sushi rolls and serve immediately.

 TIP: Eat them with chopsticks!

SOUNDS FISHY

What is sushi? Although today sushi is a typical Japanese dish, it is said to have originated in China between the third and fifth centuries BCE. It is prepared with small rolls of vinegared rice and various raw fish, such as tuna or salmon. Sushi first appeared in Japan in the eighth century as a way to preserve food such as fish in salt. Back then, sushi was mostly eaten during feast days and festivals and was a big part of these celebrations.

Now that you have a bit of sushi history under your belt, let's get to how to make basic sushi.

HOW TO MAKE SUSHI

Ingredients

5 sheets nori seaweed

1 cup (165 g) sushi rice, cooked following the package directions

8 ounces (227 g) protein of choice (such as cooked salmon, chicken, or tofu), thinly sliced

1 avocado or ½ cucumber, thinly sliced

Soy sauce, for serving

Wasabi, for serving

Sushi Preparation

1. Place the nori on a bamboo sushi mat with the shiny side facing downward.

2. Spread a thin layer of rice on the nori, leaving about 1 inch (2.5 cm) of space at the top. Wet your hands so the rice doesn't stick to your fingers.

3. Add your protein of choice and avocado or cucumber and roll up tightly.

4. Slice with a sharp knife into smaller pieces, then enjoy with soy sauce and wasabi for dipping.

COOKING SUSHI RICE

1. In a saucepan, add 1 cup (165 g) rinsed sushi rice and 1½ cups (360 ml) water and bring to a boil over medium heat. Then reduce the heat and cook until all of the water has been absorbed and the rice is tender, 15 to 20 minutes. Transfer to a large bowl.

2. In a separate saucepan over medium heat, combine ¼ cup (60 ml) rice vinegar, 1½ teaspoons vegetable oil, 2 tablespoons (25 g) sugar, and 1 teaspoon salt and cook until the sugar has dissolved. Remove from the heat and let cool.

3. Pour the vinegar mixture over the rice and stir until the rice absorbs the mixture.

ZUCCHINI FRIES

 Total Time: 17 minutes   Makes: 4 servings

Ingredients

2 medium zucchini

½ cup (60 g) all-purpose flour

2 large eggs, lightly beaten

1 cup (115 g) panko
bread crumbs

½ cup (60 g) grated
Parmesan cheese

1 tablespoon (6 g)
Italian seasoning

2 teaspoons garlic powder

½ teaspoon salt

¼ teaspoon black pepper

Nonstick cooking spray

Directions

1   Trim off the ends of the zucchini and cut each in half lengthwise. Slice the zucchini halves into ½-inch-thick (13 mm) fries.

2   Use three separate small bowls to divide the ingredients. Place the flour in the first bowl and the eggs to the second bowl. Combine the bread crumbs, Parmesan cheese, Italian seasoning, garlic powder, salt, and pepper in the third bowl.

3   First, coat each zucchini fry in the flour, gently tapping off any excess flour. Next, dip each one into the egg mixture, followed by the bread crumb mixture.

4   Preheat an air fryer at 400°F (205°C). Then arrange the fries in a single layer in an air fryer basket, leaving a little space in between each fry for the air to circulate. Spray the tops of the fries with nonstick cooking spray and air-fry at 400°F (205°C) for 12 minutes, or until the outsides are browned and crispy and the insides are tender. Cook in batches as needed. No need to flip the fries. Serve immediately.

CARROT HUMMUS

 Total Time: 15 minutes   Makes: 2 servings

Ingredients

2 cups (180 g)
chopped carrots

1 (15-ounce or 425-g)
can chickpeas

2 tablespoons (30 ml) olive oil

3 tablespoons (45 ml) tahini

1 clove garlic, crushed

2 teaspoons lemon juice

1 teaspoon ground cumin

Salt and black pepper,
to taste

Crackers and/or sliced
vegetables, for serving

Directions

1 Bring a medium saucepan of water to a boil over high heat, add the carrots and boil until soft, about 10 minutes. Drain and set aside.

2 Drain the chickpeas in a sieve set over a small bowl to collect the chickpea liquid (also called aquafaba).

3 In a blender, add the carrots, chickpeas, 2 tablespoons (30 ml) of the chickpea liquid, the olive oil, tahini, garlic, lemon juice, cumin, and salt and pepper. Blend for 2 to 3 minutes, until thick and creamy.

4 Serve with your favorite crackers and/or vegetables.

FUN FACT

Carrots were not originally colored orange. Purple, white, and yellow carrots were common thousands of years ago. Dutch horticulturists began breeding orange carrots in the 1600s.

DIP INTO YOUR FAVORITE HUMMUS

Hummus is a staple in Middle Eastern, Mediterranean, and North African cuisines and is a very popular dip for all sorts of foods. You'll typically see it as part of snack boards or appetizers. So, what is hummus? Hummus is a creamy puree of chickpeas, tahini (sesame paste), garlic, and lemon juice. Nowadays, you will find many variations and flavors of this dip. Here are three different flavors you can make at home.

PICK YOUR FLAVOR

a. Beet
b. Green pea
c. Turmeric

MAKE THE HUMMUS

Ingredients

1 (15-ounce, or 425-g) can chickpeas
2 tablespoons (30 ml) olive oil
3 tablespoons (45 ml) tahini
1 clove garlic, crushed
2 teaspoons lemon juice
Salt and black pepper, to taste

CREATE YOUR FLAVOR

Beet Flavor

1 (15-ounce, or 425-g) can cooked beets or 1 beet, cooked and sliced

1. Drain the chickpeas in a sieve set over a small bowl to collect the chickpea liquid and set aside.

2. In a blender, add the chickpeas, beet chunks, 2 tablespoons (30 ml) of the chickpea liquid, the olive oil, tahini, garlic, lemon juice, and salt and pepper. Blend for 2 to 3 minutes, until thick and creamy.

Green Pea Flavor

1 (15-ounce, or 425-g) can green peas

1. Drain the chickpeas in a sieve set over a small bowl to collect the chickpea liquid and set aside.

2. In a blender, add the chickpeas, green peas, 2 tablespoons (30 ml) of the chickpea liquid, the olive oil, garlic, and salt and pepper. Do not include the tahini and lemon juice. Blend for 2 to 3 minutes, until thick and creamy.

Turmeric Flavor

1 tablespoon turmeric
1 teaspoon paprika
2 tablespoons (30 ml) sesame oil

1. Drain the chickpeas in a sieve set over a small bowl to collect the chickpea liquid and set aside.

2. In a blender, add the chickpeas, turmeric, paprika, sesame oil, 2 tablespoons (30 ml) of the chickpea liquid, the olive oil, tahini, garlic, lemon juice, and salt and pepper. Blend for 2 to 3 minutes, until thick and creamy.

PEAR & APPLE NACHOS

 Total Time: 10 minutes   Makes: 2 servings

Ingredients

1 pear of choice, sliced

1 apple of choice, sliced

⅓ cup (80 ml) almond butter

2 tablespoons (10 g) shredded coconut

⅓ cup (50 g) sliced almonds

2 tablespoons (20 g) chocolate chips

2 tablespoons (15 g) golden raisins

Directions

1 Spread the pear and apple slices on a large plate.

2 In a small microwave-safe bowl, add the almond butter and melt in the microwave for 30 to 45 seconds, then let cool slightly. Use a spoon to drizzle the almond butter over the top of the pears and apples.

3 Top with the shredded coconut, sliced almonds, chocolate chips, and golden raisins.

✳ **TIP:** You can switch any of the toppings for others you might enjoy more, like caramel sauce, chocolate sauce, or peanut butter.

FUN FACT

Did you know that Alexander the Great, the king of ancient Greece, is credited with discovering apples? Or that pears can grow on trees that live for at least a hundred years? Or that pears can be traced back to 1000 BCE?

MINI PRETZEL TWISTS

 Total Time: 20 minutes   Makes: 60 mini pretzels

Ingredients

Nonstick cooking spray

1 (13.8-ounce or 391-g) can refrigerated classic pizza crust (such as Pillsbury)

⅓ cup (90 g) baking soda

1 egg, slightly beaten

2 teaspoons (12 g) kosher salt

Directions

1   Preheat the oven to 450°F (230°C) for 10 minutes. Spray a baking sheet with nonstick cooking spray and set aside.

2   Unroll the pizza dough on a cutting board and cut it into 3 x ½-inch (7.5 x 1.3 cm) strips. Roll each strip into a rope about 5 inches (12.5 cm) long, then cross one end of the dough strip over the other end and poke it underneath. Hold on to both ends and pull to tie into a knot.

3   In a medium saucepan over high heat, bring 5 cups (1.4 L) of water and the baking soda to a boil. Drop the dough knots, 6 at a time, into the boiling water and cook for 30 seconds. Remove the knots with a slotted spoon and place on the prepared baking sheet about ½ inch (13 mm) apart.

4   Brush the dough with the beaten egg and sprinkle with the salt.

5   Bake for 10 minutes, or until golden brown. Transfer to a wire rack and let cool.

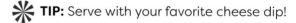 **TIP:** Serve with your favorite cheese dip!

SPREAD THE FOOD LOVE

Snack boards are gaining popularity in many homes, especially during celebrations. It allows people to share food while also trying delicious new options. Boards can include anything you want! Experiment with new snacks and get creative with some of your favorites by making cute shapes.

First, decide whether you want to create a sweet or savory snack spread or a combination of both. Next, ask yourself how many people the snack board is for. These questions will help you figure out how much and what to add to your spread. Here are a few tips for preparing your snack spread:

1. Gather your board and all the ingredients you will be using.
2. Place serving bowls on the board before adding any foods.
3. Cut any food that needs to be sliced, such as cheeses, certain large fruits, and veggies. This is where you can get creative and make cool shapes out of your snacks.
4. Start by placing the larger pieces of food first and then add your smaller items.

CREATING YOUR VERY OWN SNACK SPREAD

The easiest spread you can make is one that uses what you already have in your kitchen and in your fridge. Look for some of your favorite things or leftovers that you may have and start to gather your favorites together. Here I've compiled an example spread you can do at home to share. Swap foods that you don't have or don't want to include with any of your personal favorites.

Ingredients

¾ cup (180 ml) ranch or
blue cheese dressing

½ cup (120 ml) peanut butter

1 cup (120 g) baby carrots

6 ribs celery, sliced into thirds

1 cup (120 g) cheddar cheese
cubes or shapes

1 small bunch green or red grapes

12 crackers

10 to 12 chocolate-covered pretzels

6 to 10 granola bars

½ red apple, sliced

12 whole strawberries

2 mandarin oranges, peeled and separated

1 cup (16 g) popped popcorn

Snack Spread Preparation

1. Place the ranch and peanut butter in serving bowls and position on the board.

2. Arrange the carrots and celery sticks around the dressing and peanut butter.

3. Place the cheese shapes around the board and any cubes on the center on the board.

4. Arrange the grapes and then add the crackers, pretzels, and granola bars.

5. Arrange the apple slices, strawberries, and oranges around any open space. Add the popcorn in a bowl and add to the spread.

SWEET POTATO CHIPS

 Total Time: 15 minutes   Makes: 2 servings

Ingredients

1 large sweet potato
Salt, to taste

Directions

1   Peel the sweet potato. Using a mandoline peeler, slice it into thin pieces. Please ask an adult to help with this as a mandoline peeler can be tough to work with, and use caution.

2   Place the slices on a large microwave-safe plate that can fit in a microwave and sprinkle with salt.

3   Microwave for 45 seconds, flip, and microwave for another 45 seconds. The chips will begin to brown. Continue to microwave in 30-second intervals until cooked to your desired crispiness. Let cool.

FUN FACT

Sweet potatoes have high levels of dietary fiber, potassium, iron, and vitamins A and C. They are the number one most nutritional vegetable, even more than greens like broccoli or spinach, so make this recipe often.

AIR FRYER PASTA CHIPS

 Total Time: 16 minutes   Makes: 8 servings

Ingredients

2 cups (200 g) farfalle
(bow tie) pasta

1 tablespoon (15 ml) olive oil

½ cup (60 g) grated
Parmesan cheese

1 teaspoon garlic powder

1 teaspoon Italian seasoning

½ teaspoon salt

Directions

1 Bring a large pot of water to a boil over high heat, add the pasta and cook, stirring occasionally, until tender yet firm, about 8 minutes. Drain the pasta but do not rinse.

2 Preheat an air fryer to 400°F (205°C) for 3 minutes. Transfer the cooked pasta to a large bowl and drizzle with the olive oil. Add the Parmesan cheese, garlic powder, Italian seasoning, and salt and stir until the pasta is thoroughly coated.

3 Arrange ¼ cup (25 g) of the pasta in a single layer in the air fryer basket. Cook for 5 minutes, flip, and cook for another 2 to 3 minutes. Transfer to a paper towel-lined plate. Repeat this step with the remaining pasta until all is cooked.

4 Pull apart any pasta chips that have stuck together and let them cool completely before eating.

 **TIP:** Serve with marinara sauce.

PAPER BAG POPCORN

 Total Time: 5 minutes   Makes: 2 cups (32 g)

Ingredients

⅓ cup (80 g) popcorn kernels

1 medium (13⅜ H x 6⁵⁄₁₆ W x 4³⁄₁₆-inch D) brown paper bag

Salt, to taste

Directions

1 Add the popcorn kernels to the paper bag and fold the top over. Microwave on high for 1 minute and 45 seconds.

2 Dump the popped popcorn into a large bowl and season with salt.

 TIP: Add butter while the popcorn is still warm to make movie theater–style popcorn.

HOW TO MAKE SWEET POPCORN

1 Add the popcorn kernels to the paper bag and fold the top over. Microwave on high for 1 minute and 45 seconds.

2 Dump the popped popcorn into a large bowl and set aside.

3 In a medium bowl, combine 2 tablespoons (30 ml) melted butter, 2 tablespoons (30 ml) honey or golden syrup, and 2 tablespoons (25 g) brown sugar.

4 Pour the mixture on top of the popcorn and toss to thoroughly coat.

TIP: You can swap out the brown sugar for granulated sugar and add 2 teaspoons ground cinnamon and ½ teaspoon vanilla extract for a different flavor.

CHEESE CRACKERS

 Total Time: 52 minutes Makes: 64 crackers

Ingredients

1 cup (120 g) shredded cheddar cheese

¼ cup (30 g) grated Parmesan cheese

¼ cup (½ stick or 55 g) unsalted butter

¾ cup (90 g) all-purpose flour, plus more for dusting

¼ teaspoon salt

Nonstick cooking spray

Directions

1 In a food processor, add the cheddar cheese, Parmesan cheese, butter, flour, and salt and pulse until a dough ball forms. Wrap the dough in plastic wrap and refrigerate for 30 minutes.

2 Meanwhile, preheat the oven to 350°F (175°C). Spray a baking sheet with nonstick cooking spray and set aside.

3 On a lightly floured surface, roll out the dough using a lightly floured rolling pin into a 6-inch (15 cm) square. With a knife, cut the dough into 1-inch (2.5 cm) squares. Place on the prepared baking sheet.

4 Bake for 15 minutes, or until desired crunchiness is achieved. Transfer to a wire rack and let cool completely.

TIP: Use a small vegetable cutter to cut out the dough in fun shapes!

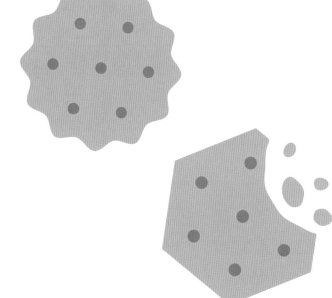

FUN FACT
Cheddar cheese is one of the best sources of calcium.

DESSERTS

COCONUT SORBET

 Total Time: 5 hours and 25 minutes   Makes: 10 servings

Ingredients

1 cup (240 ml) coconut water

½ cup (100 g) sugar

2 (13.5-ounce or 400-ml) cans unsweetened coconut milk, chilled

1 (13.5-ounce or 400-ml) can unsweetened coconut cream, chilled

Shredded coconut or coconut flakes, for topping

Sprinkles, for topping

Directions

1 In a small saucepan over low heat, add the coconut water and sugar. Cook until the sugar dissolves. Remove from the heat and transfer the mixture to the refrigerator so that it can cool completely.

2 Remove the mixture from the fridge and add to a blender. Pour in the coconut milk and coconut cream and blend just until the mixture is well combined.

3 Pour the mixture into a 9 x 5-inch (23 x 12.5 cm) metal baking pan. Freeze until firm, about 5 hours. Stir the sorbet every 30 minutes with a fork for the first 3 hours to prevent any large ice crystals from forming.

4 Top with shredded coconut and sprinkles, if desired.

 TIPS: A small saucepan is best when cooking sugar because the sugar may cook too quickly and even overcook in a large pot. Top the sorbet with confetti sprinkles to make it more fun!

PEANUT BUTTER YOGURT BARK

 Total Time: 4 hours and 15 minutes   Makes: 10 servings

Ingredients

1½ cups (360 ml) plain Greek yogurt

½ cup (120 ml) peanut butter

2 tablespoons (30 ml) honey or maple syrup

½ cup (85 g) semisweet chocolate chips

Directions

1   Line a baking sheet with parchment paper.

2   In a large bowl, add the Greek yogurt, peanut butter, and honey and stir until well combined. Spread the mixture evenly over the prepared baking sheet.

3   In a small microwave-safe bowl, melt the chocolate chips in the microwave in 30-second intervals, stirring after each interval, until smooth.

4   Using a spoon, add dollops of melted chocolate to the yogurt mixture, and with a toothpick, gently swirl the chocolate into the yogurt mixture.

5   Freeze the bark for at least 4 hours, or until hardened. Cut into pieces to serve.

 TIP: Top with slices of banana, graham cracker crumbs, sprinkles, or even chopped nuts for other flavor options.

NO-BAKE FAVORITES!

Here are some more no-bake desserts that you can make easily at home.

Banana Split

This is a classic as far as American desserts go, and very simple to make. It is a hit at most parties and celebrations. If you're in the mood for some ice cream, make yourself a banana split.

1 medium banana

1 scoop vanilla ice cream

1 scoop chocolate ice cream

1 scoop strawberry ice cream

2 tablespoons (18 g) sliced fresh strawberries

2 tablespoons (18 g) pineapple chunks

2 tablespoons (10 g) whipped cream

1 tablespoon (9 g) chopped peanuts

1 tablespoon (15 ml) chocolate syrup

2 Maraschino cherries

1. Peel and slice the banana lengthwise. Place the banana, cut sides up, on a dessert dish.

2. Add the scoops of vanilla, chocolate, and strawberry ice cream in between the banana slices.

3. Add the strawberry slices and pineapple chunks on top of the ice cream.

4. Top with the whipped cream, chopped peanuts, chocolate syrup, and cherries.

Confetti Dip

This dip is perfect for birthday parties and celebrations. You can enjoy it with animal crackers, Oreos, or any of your favorite cookies. This makes 15 servings.

4 cups (432 g) confetti cake mix (such as Funfetti)

1 (8-ounce or 227-g) container frozen whipped topping (such as Cool Whip)

1½ cups (360 ml) vanilla yogurt

Sprinkles

1. In a medium bowl, mix together the cake mix, whipped topping, and vanilla yogurt for about 2 minutes, or until well combined.

2. Transfer the dip to a serving bowl and refrigerate, uncovered, for 15 minutes.

3. Remove the mixture from the refrigerator and top with sprinkles.

4. Serve with your favorite cookies.

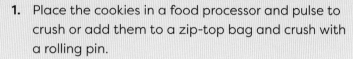

Sandwich Cookie Balls

This is a simple and delicious recipe that will certainly win over guests, family, and friends. This makes about 28 balls.

1 (36-count) pack sandwich cookies (such as Oreos)

1 (8-ounce or 227-g) package cream cheese, at room temperature

1 (16-ounce or 454-g) bag semisweet chocolate chips

1. Place the cookies in a food processor and pulse to crush or add them to a zip-top bag and crush with a rolling pin.

2. In a medium or large bowl, combine the cookie crumbs and cream cheese until well combined.

3. Shape the cream cheese mixture into 1-inch (2.5 cm) balls and place on a baking sheet lined with parchment paper. Be sure to keep the balls far enough apart that they don't stick together. Transfer the balls to the freezer and freeze for 10 to 15 minutes.

4. In a medium microwave-safe bowl, melt the chocolate chips in the microwave in 15-second intervals, stirring after each interval, until fully melted and smooth. Let the chocolate cool for 1 to 2 minutes before removing from the microwave.

5. Remove the balls from the freezer and line a shallow pan with parchment paper.

6. Using a fork or toothpick, dip the balls one at a time into the melted chocolate and place them in the pan. Refrigerate for 1 hour, or until firm.

PRETZEL CHOCOLATE FLOWERS

 Total Time: 12 minutes   Makes: 15 servings

Ingredients

15 square pretzels

1 (12-ounce or 340-g) bag white candy melts (such as Wilton brand)

1 (10-ounce or 283-g) bag candy-coated chocolates (such as M&M's)

Directions

1   Preheat the oven to 250°F (120°C). Line a baking sheet with parchment paper.

2   Arrange the pretzels on the prepared baking sheet. Place 2 candy melts on top of each pretzel and bake for 2 to 3 minutes until melted. Remove from the oven.

3   While the candy melts are still warm, place 1 candy-coated chocolate in the center of each pretzel, pressing down and spreading the candy melts. Place 6 candy-coated chocolates around the center for the petals of the flower. Allow to set completely before moving, about 15 minutes.

 TIP: Get creative and have fun with this recipe! Place one color for the center and different colors for the petals.

FUN FACT

Eating pure cocoa or dark chocolate is good for your teeth health, in that it can prevent tooth decay.

CHOCOLATE DIRT CUPS

 Total Time: 40 minutes Makes: 8 servings

Ingredients

2 cups (480 ml) cold milk

2 (3.4-ounce or 96-g) boxes instant chocolate pudding mix

1 cup (120 ml) whipped cream

12 chocolate sandwich cookies (such as Oreos)

Directions

1 In a large bowl, add the milk and pudding mixture and whisk until the powder completely dissolves.

2 Place the pudding in the refrigerator for 10 minutes, then remove from the refrigerator and fold the whipped cream into the chocolate pudding, mixing well.

3 Spoon the pudding into clear cups and place back in the refrigerator for at least 20 minutes to chill and set further.

4 Place cookies in a zip-top bag and roll over them with a rolling pin to crush them.

5 Remove the cups from the refrigerator and sprinkle the cookie crumbs on top of each cup.

 TIP: Add gummy worms for a fun, spooky treat!

A CHOCOLATEY HISTORY

Let's talk about one of the best-loved foods in the world—chocolate! Where does it come from? Well, it is the fruit of the cacao tree, native to Central and South America, and can be traced back to the ancient Mayans. The fruits are called pods and each one has about forty cacao beans in it.

The cacao beans have to be dried and roasted. There is no clear origin as to who exactly invented chocolate. However, we do know that the sweet chocolate that we enjoy today is not the same as the chocolate many enjoyed throughout history.

Chocolate was first a bitter and spicy beverage and did not gain popularity until it started to be enjoyed in the royal courts of Europe and colonial America. Before that, chocolate was sacred in Mayan culture and consumed during celebrations and in completing important transactions. Although chocolate was mainly for the rich and powerful, many Mayan households included chocolate in their everyday meals. Similarly to the Mayans, the Aztecs revered chocolate,

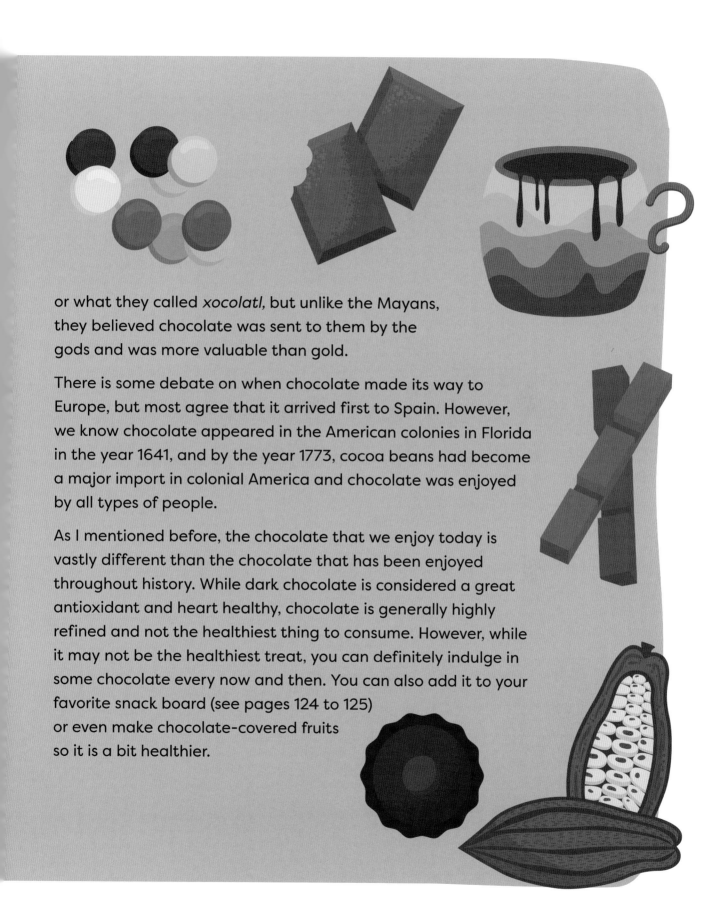

or what they called *xocolatl,* but unlike the Mayans, they believed chocolate was sent to them by the gods and was more valuable than gold.

There is some debate on when chocolate made its way to Europe, but most agree that it arrived first to Spain. However, we know chocolate appeared in the American colonies in Florida in the year 1641, and by the year 1773, cocoa beans had become a major import in colonial America and chocolate was enjoyed by all types of people.

As I mentioned before, the chocolate that we enjoy today is vastly different than the chocolate that has been enjoyed throughout history. While dark chocolate is considered a great antioxidant and heart healthy, chocolate is generally highly refined and not the healthiest thing to consume. However, while it may not be the healthiest treat, you can definitely indulge in some chocolate every now and then. You can also add it to your favorite snack board (see pages 124 to 125) or even make chocolate-covered fruits so it is a bit healthier.

WAFFLE COOKIES

 Total Time: 20 minutes   Makes: 28 cookies

Ingredients

1½ cups (180 g) all-purpose flour

1 teaspoon baking powder

½ teaspoon salt

½ cup (1 stick or 115 g) unsalted butter, at room temperature

½ cup (100 g) granulated sugar

½ cup (110 g) packed light brown sugar

2 large eggs, at room temperature

1 teaspoon vanilla extract

1 cup (120 g) confectioners' sugar, for topping

Directions

1 Preheat a waffle iron for 5 minutes.

2 In a large bowl, combine the flour, baking powder, and salt. Set aside.

3 Using an electric mixer on medium speed, beat the butter, granulated sugar, and brown sugar until light and fluffy. Add the eggs, one at a time, and beat just until well combined. Add the vanilla and beat to combine.

4 Slowly add the flour mixture to the egg mixture slowly and beat to combine, scraping down the side of the bowl as needed.

5 Scoop 1 tablespoon (15 g) of the cookie dough mixture into the waffle iron. Close the iron and cook for about 2 minutes. Remove and let cool for 5 minutes. Repeat with the remaining dough.

6 Sprinkle each cookie with the confectioners' sugar before serving.

TWO-INGREDIENT RED VELVET CAKE

 Total Time: 45 minutes   Makes: 16 servings

Ingredients

Baking spray

1 store-bought red velvet cake mix (such as Betty Crocker Delights)

1 (12-ounce or 355-ml) can diet dark soda (such as Dr Pepper)

Directions

1   Preheat the oven to 350°F (175°C) for 10 minutes. Grease an 8 x 8-inch (20 x 20 cm) baking dish with baking spray.

2   In a large bowl, stir together the red velvet cake mix and the can of dark soda until no large lumps are visible. Pour the batter into the prepared pan.

3   Bake for 35 to 40 minutes, until a knife inserted into the center comes out clean. Transfer to a wire rack and let cool for 20 minutes.

※ **TIP:** Top the cake with whipped cream and sprinkles!

HOW TO MAKE EASY CREAM CHEESE FROSTING
(makes 2 cups or 480 g)

1 Using an electric mixer on medium speed, combine 8 ounces (227 g) cream cheese, ½ cup (1 stick or 115 g) unsalted butter, and 2 teaspoons vanilla extract. Beat until light and creamy, about 5 minutes.

2 Slowly add in 4 cups (480 g) confectioners' sugar and beat until smooth.

CAKEALICIOUS

If you want to try to make a cake from scratch instead of from a box, you've come to the right place. Here I will share an easy recipe. But first, there is some equipment you will need to bake your cake:

- 13 x 9-inch (33 x 23 cm) metal baking pan
- Measuring cups
- Measuring spoons
- Medium or large mixing bowl
- Stand mixer, hand mixer, or whisk

- Toothpick
- Oven mitts
- Wire rack
- Offset spatula or spoon
- Chef's knife

MAKE THE CAKE

Baking spray
1½ cups (300 g) sugar
1¼ cups (150 g) all-purpose flour
1 teaspoon baking powder
½ teaspoon baking soda
½ teaspoon salt
1 cup (2 sticks, or 225 g) unsalted butter, at room temperature

1 teaspoon vanilla extract
1¼ cups (300 ml) milk (whole or 2%), divided
⅔ cup (165 ml) vegetable oil
3 large eggs
1 (16-ounce or 454-g) container vanilla or chocolate frosting (such as Betty Crocker)

1. Preheat the oven to 350°F (175°C). Spray the bottoms and sides of a 13 x 9-inch (33 x 23 cm) metal baking pan with baking spray and set aside.

2. In a large mixing bowl or using a stand mixer, sift together the sugar, flour, baking powder, baking soda, and salt. Whisk on low speed for 15 seconds to combine. Add the butter, vanilla, and ½ cup (120 ml) of the milk and mix on medium speed until moistened, about 1 minute. Scrape down the sides and bottom of the bowl.

3. In a medium bowl, whisk the remaining ¾ cup (180 ml) milk, oil, and eggs until smooth, about 30 seconds. Then add the milk mixture in three additions to the dry mixture, whisking on medium speed for 15 seconds after each addition. Stop the mixer and scrape the bottom of the bowl, then mix for an additional 15 to 30 seconds, until the batter is completely combined.

4. Pour the batter into the prepared pan and spread evenly. Bake for 32 to 35 minutes, until a toothpick inserted into the center of the cake comes out clean or with a few crumbs.

5. Transfer to a wire rack and let cool completely. Ask an adult for help with this if the pan is too heavy.

6. Spread the frosting on the cake using an offset spatula or a spoon.

Have Some Fun Decorating Your Cake
Here are a few quick tips for decorating your cake.

1. Add sprinkles on top of your frosting—this can be a specific color (different from the frosting on the cake) or rainbow sprinkles. This is a simple way to add some visual creativity to your cake.

2. Top your cake with cookie crumbs, shredded coconut, or chocolate chips.

3. Add some fruits, such as berries or sliced strawberries, nuts, or candies!

4. Pipe on different designs, such as simple lines, names, balloons, and polka dots; you can do what you want here! Use a different color frosting than what you used to cover the cake and add it to a small zip-top bag. Cut the corner of the bag using scissors so you have a small opening. Squeeze small amounts of frosting as you create the design you want. This takes practice but is tons of fun! It's a great thing to do with an adult or friends.

S'MORES BARS

 Total Time: 26 minutes   Makes: 16 bars

Ingredients

Baking spray

2 cups (200 g) graham cracker crumbs

½ cup (60 g) confectioners' sugar

½ cup (1 stick or 115 g) unsalted butter, melted

4 (4.4-ounce or 125-g) chocolate bars

1 (16-ounce or 454-g) package mini marshmallows

Directions

1   Preheat the oven to 350°F (175°C). Grease an 8 x 8-inch (20 x 20 cm) baking dish with baking spray.

2   In a medium bowl, mix together the graham cracker crumbs, confectioners' sugar, and melted butter until combined well. Spread the mixture in the bottom of the prepared baking pan and press down evenly.

3   Bake for 6 minutes, then remove from the oven and let cool. Keep the oven on.

4   Once cool, lay the chocolate bars on top of the graham cracker mixture, covering it completely. Place back in the oven for 3 minutes, then remove and let cool for 2 minutes. Scatter the marshmallows on top of the chocolate.

5   Turn the oven to high broil and put the pan in the oven. Check frequently because the marshmallows can burn quickly. Remove the pan as soon as the marshmallows begin to brown. Transfer to a wire rack and let cool completely.

COOKIE BAKE

 Total Time: 40 minutes Makes: 12 servings

Ingredients

Baking spray

½ cup (1 stick or 115 g) unsalted butter, at room temperature

½ cup (110 g) golden brown sugar, packed

½ cup (100 g) granulated sugar

1 teaspoon vanilla extract

½ teaspoon salt

2 large eggs

1½ cups (180 g) all-purpose flour

½ teaspoon baking soda

1½ cups (285 g) semisweet chocolate chips, plus more for topping

Directions

1 Preheat the oven to 350°F (175°C). Coat an 8 x 8-inch (20 x 20 cm) baking dish with baking spray and set aside.

2 In a hand mixer, add the butter, brown sugar, and granulated sugar and beat until light and fluffy. Add the vanilla, salt, and eggs, one at a time, and continue mixing, scraping down the sides of the bowl if necessary. Mix in the flour and baking soda. Add the chocolate chips and give a final stir.

3 Press the cookie dough into the prepared baking dish and top with more chocolate chips.

4 Bake for 30 minutes, or until the edges are golden brown. Transfer to a wire rack to cool. The cookie bars will continue to cook as they cool.

VANILLA MUG CAKE

 Total Time: 5 minutes   Makes: 1 serving

Ingredients

¼ cup (30 g) all-purpose flour

2 tablespoons (25 g) sugar

¼ teaspoon baking powder

Pinch of salt

3 tablespoons (45 ml) milk

2 tablespoons (28 g) unsalted butter, melted

½ teaspoon vanilla extract

1 teaspoon sprinkles

Directions

1 In a large mug, mix the flour, sugar, baking powder, and salt until well combined. Stir in the milk, melted butter, and vanilla until smooth. Scrape the bottom of the mug and stir in the sprinkles.

2 Cook in a microwave for 1 minute and 10 seconds to 1 minute and 30 seconds, until the cake is just set but still shiny on top.

3 Let the mug cake rest in the microwave for 1 minute before eating.

 TIP: Stir in a handful of chocolate chips in Step 1 for a fun chocolate twist!

FUN FACT

The oldest-known cake in the world dates to 2200 BCE and was found in the Egyptian tomb of Pepionkh. It can be found in the Alimentarium Food Museum in Switzerland.

EXTRA-FUDGY BROWNIES

 Total Time: 30 minutes   Makes: 12 brownies

Ingredients

Baking spray

1½ cups (300 g) sugar

½ cup (1 stick or 115 g) unsalted butter, melted and cooled

½ teaspoon vanilla extract

2 eggs, at room temperature

¾ cup (90 g) all-purpose flour, plus 1 teaspoon for the chocolate chips

½ cup (45 g) unsweetened cocoa powder

¼ teaspoon salt

¼ teaspoon baking soda

1 cup (165 g) semisweet chocolate chips

Directions

1 Preheat the oven to 350°F (175°C). Grease an 8 x 8-inch (20 x 20 cm) baking dish with baking spray and set aside.

2 In a large bowl, add the sugar, butter, and vanilla and stir until smooth. Add the eggs, one at a time, and stir after each addition until well combined.

3 In a separate large bowl, stir together the ¾ cup (90 g) flour, cocoa powder, salt, and baking soda. Add the flour mixture slowly to the sugar and butter mixture and stir until well combined.

4 In a small bowl, toss the chocolate chips with the remaining 1 teaspoon flour, then add them to the batter. (This helps prevent them from sinking to the bottom.)

5 Pour the batter into the prepared baking dish and bake for 20 to 25 minutes, until the edges start to pull away from the sides of the pan. The center may look slightly jiggly, but it will firm up once the brownies have cooled. Serve warm.

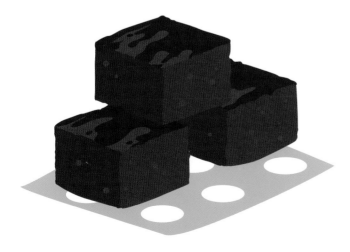

SMOOTHIES
& FRESH JUICES

GREEN LEMONADE

 Total Time: 8 minutes   Makes: 2 servings

Ingredients

2 green apples

½ cup (120 ml) cold water

1 lemon

¾ cup (180 ml) sparkling water or seltzer

Ice cubes

1½ teaspoons sugar

1 small bunch fresh mint

Directions

1 Cut the apples into ½-inch (13 mm) chunks, making sure to remove the core.

2 In a blender, add the apple chunks and water and blend until smooth. Pour the apple mixture into a pitcher.

3 Slice the lemon in half and, using a juicer or sieve to catch the seeds, squeeze the juice onto the apple juice mixture. Add the sparkling water, ice, and sugar, stirring well.

4 Pour the juice into two glasses, garnish with mint leaves, and serve.

HOW TO MAKE CLASSIC LEMONADE

1 Using a cutting board and a sharp knife, cut 10 lemons in half.

2 Using a juicer or sieve, squeeze each half of the lemon over a medium bowl. Be sure to get as much juice as possible, about 1¾ cups (420 ml) to 2 cups (480 ml).

3 In a large pitcher, mix 6 cups (1.4 L) water, the lemon juice, and 1 cup (200 g) sugar and stir until the sugar is dissolved. Refrigerate for about 3 hours.

4 Serve the lemonade over ice and garnish with a lemon slice.

A LEMONADE TWIST ON HISTORY

Who doesn't love a nice cold glass of lemonade, especially during those scorching summer months? Most of us have had a glass once or twice in our lives. Lemonade is a classic drink that has been around for thousands of years. In fact, the first record of lemonade comes from twelfth-century Egypt. So, it's safe to say that it is a drink that has been around a long time, and by now there are many variations of it. In its simplest form, lemonade is a mix of water, sugar, and fresh lemon juice.

Lemonade first made its appearance in Europe in 1630. During this time, lemonade was made by mixing sparkling water, lemon juice, and honey. It became so popular in Paris that in 1676 vendors created a union called *Compagnie de Limonadiers.* In the 1780s, Johann Schweppe, a German-Swiss jeweler, made the mass production of lemonade much easier by inventing a new method of carbonating water.

With the mass production of lemonade and the arrival of European immigrants to America, it wasn't too long before this classic drink made its debut in America in the eighteenth century. During the Victorian era, the Women's Christian Temperance Movement pushed abstinence from alcohol and advocated for lemonade as an alternative drink. In the 1870s, lemonade became a popular drink among elites when First Lady Lucy Ware convinced her husband, President Rutherford Hayes, to ban alcohol in the White House.

Nowadays, lemonade is a popular drink in most restaurants and bars. No matter how you drink this delicious concoction, it's fair to say that lemonade has a fascinating history and is one of the most popular drinks around.

DIFFERENT FLAVORS OF LEMONADE

As I mentioned earlier, nowadays you can find many variations of lemonade flavors and colors. Lemonade is more often than not a combination of water, sugar, and lemon juice. However, you can always spice it up by swapping out the water for coconut water and adding other fruit flavors. Here is a list of some of the more common flavors beyond the classic that can be easily made at home.

- **Pink lemonade:** Although its origin is debated, this drink can be made with pink or red dye. If you want to keep it natural, you can make this drink using grenadine, cranberry juice, or strawberry puree.

- **Blueberry lemonade:** This delicious concoction can be made, just as the name suggests, with the addition of blueberry puree.

- **Strawberry lemonade:** This lemonade can be made with (you guessed it!) the addition of strawberry puree.

- **Pineapple-mango lemonade:** This lemonade can be made with the addition of pineapple and mango juices, and pineapple and mango chunks for an added natural flavor.

- **Peach lemonade:** This delicious drink can be made with the addition of peach slices.

KOOL-AID COOL KID SLUSHIE

 Total Time: 4 minutes   Makes: 2 servings

Ingredients

1 (0.13-ounce or 3.6-g) packet Kool-Aid flavor of choice

½ cup (100 g) sugar

5 cups (1200 g) ice cubes

2 cups (480 ml) cold water

Directions

1 In a blender, add the Kool-Aid packet, sugar, ice, and water. Blend in 15-second intervals until it turns into a slushy consistency.

2 Pour into two glasses and serve.

✳ **TIP:** Replace the water with club soda to make it fizzy!

MAKE CUSTOMIZED FRUIT SLUSHIES

1 Chop 1½ cups (about 225 g) of your desired fruit (this can include strawberries, blueberries, oranges, pineapples, watermelon, and more). You can mix and match fruits or just chop one fruit of choice.

2 Mix the chopped fruit with 1 cup (240 g) ice cubes in a blender and blend on high speed until the mixture is the consistency of a slushie.

STRAWBERRY REFRESHER

 Total Time: 7 minutes   Makes: 6 servings

Ingredients

2½ teaspoons freeze-dried strawberry powder

1 teaspoon freeze-dried acaí powder

3 cups (720 ml) cold water, divided

2 teaspoons passion fruit puree, plus more if needed

2½ cups (600 ml) white grape juice

Ice cubes

½ cup (72 g) freeze-dried strawberries

Directions

1   In a pitcher, combine the strawberry powder and acaí powder with 1 cup (240 ml) of the water and stir until dissolved.

2   Slowly stir in the remaining 2 cups (480 ml) water, passion fruit puree, and white grape juice. Taste and add more passion fruit puree, ¼ teaspoon at a time, if desired.

3   Add ice and the freeze-dried strawberries to your glasses. Pour in the juice mixture and stir.

✳ **TIP:** You can swap out the freeze-dried strawberries with fresh ones for a more authentic flavor!

FUN FACT

A fruit puree is a fruit that has been cooked, ground, sieved, blended, or pressed until it reaches a creamy consistency. You can find passion fruit purees in most grocery stores, usually in the summertime, or online.

STRAWBERRY BANANA SMOOTHIE

 Total Time: 5 minutes   Makes: 2 servings

Ingredients

⅓ cup (67 g) frozen strawberries

2 frozen bananas, sliced

¾ cup (180 ml) milk (whole or 2%)

Directions

1   In a blender, add the strawberries, bananas, and milk and blend until smooth.

2   Pour into two glasses and serve.

 TIP: If lactose intolerant, you can replace the milk with water or coconut water.

BLUEBERRY SMOOTHIE

 Total Time: 5 minutes   Makes: 2 servings

Ingredients

⅓ orange, peeled, separated, and seeds removed

1 cup (150 g) blueberries

1 frozen banana

½ cup (120 ml) milk (whole or 2%)

Directions

1   In a blender, add the orange, blueberries, banana, and milk and blend until smooth.

2   Pour the smoothie into two glasses and serve.

 TIP: If lactose intolerant, you can replace the milk with water or coconut water.

PINEAPPLE MANGO MADNESS SMOOTHIE

 Total Time: 5 minutes   Makes: 2 servings

Ingredients

1 cup (165 g) frozen mango chunks

1½ cups (250 g) frozen pineapple chunks

1 large banana

4 leaves fresh mint

½ cup (120 ml) coconut water

Directions

1 In a blender, add the frozen mango and pineapple chunks, banana, mint leaves, and coconut water and blend until smooth.

2 Pour the smoothie into two glasses and serve.

※ **TIP:** Coconut water adds a wonderful burst of flavor, but it can be replaced by regular water, if desired.

BLOOD ORANGE SMOOTHIE

 Total Time: 5 minutes   Makes: 2 servings

Ingredients

2 blood oranges, peeled, separated, and seeds removed

½ cup (120 ml) cold water

1 cup (20 g) baby spinach

1½ cups (225 g) frozen mixed berries

1 frozen banana

Directions

1 In a blender, add the blood oranges, water, spinach, mixed berries, and banana and blend until smooth.

2 Pour the smoothie into two glasses and serve.

※ **TIP:** You can add 1 teaspoon of honey and 2 teaspoons of ground flaxseeds to make this smoothie more filling!

ICED MATCHA LATTE

 Total Time: 5 minutes   Makes: 2 servings

Ingredients

½ cup (15 g) fresh spinach

¾ cup (180 ml) almond milk

½ teaspoon vanilla extract

Ice cubes

Maple syrup or honey,
to taste (optional)

Directions

1 In a blender, process the spinach, milk, and vanilla until the spinach is completely blended.

2 Fill two glasses with ice cubes and pour in the "matcha" mixture, adding the maple syrup or honey, if desired.

3 Stir well before serving.

FUN FACT

A *latte* is a type of coffee drink that combines espresso and steamed milk. It got its name from the Italian word *caffé latte, caffelatte,* or *caffellatte,* which all translate to "coffee and milk."

FOR THE LOVE OF FRUITS

Fruits are great sources of minerals, vitamins, and fiber. Here I list some common fruits and their benefits.

- **Apples:** Apples have many health benefits, such as lowering blood pressure, cholesterol, and inflammation. They can also strengthen your lungs.

- **Avocado:** Avocados are great for eye health, preventing osteoporosis (a bone disease), improving digestion, and reducing the risk of depression. They are great additions to salads, sandwiches, toast, and eggs.

- **Bananas:** Bananas are great for improving metabolism, maintaining organ health, lowering blood pressure, and boosting skin and hair health.

- **Blueberries:** Blueberries are great antioxidants and anti-inflammatories.

- **Cherries:** Cherries are potent sources of fiber and potassium.

- **Coconut:** Coconuts contain many antioxidants to fight against cell damage and help control blood sugar levels.

- **Grapes:** Grapes help improve sleep, keep you hydrated, and boost your immunity, among other things.

- **Guava:** Guavas are known as a superfood and have many benefits, including helping with eyesight, reducing stress and the risk of cancer, and managing blood sugar.

- **Kiwis:** Kiwis help protect our respiratory systems, maintain our gut health, and are great for immunity and hair growth.

- **Mangoes:** Mangoes include strong antioxidants that can protect the body from chronic diseases such as heart disease, Parkinson's, and type 2 diabetes. They also contain sources of fiber to help with our digestive systems and vitamins A, C, B6, E, and K.

- **Oranges:** Oranges are a great source of vitamin C, which helps with glowing skin, fighting colds, and maintaining healthy bones and teeth.

- **Pineapples:** Pineapples are popular tropical fruits that are great for supporting your metabolism, regulating blood sugar, and are potent antioxidants.

- **Strawberries:** Strawberries are rich in nutrients and have some vitamin C and other antioxidants to reduce the risk of serious conditions such as diabetes and cancer.

- **Watermelon:** Watermelon is great for helping you stay hydrated and is highly alkalizing. It's also a great anti-inflammatory and helps prevent muscle soreness.

WHIPPED CHOCOLATE MILK

 Total Time: 22 minutes   Makes: 12 servings

Ingredients

¼ cup (30 g) confectioners' sugar

¼ cup (30 g) cocoa powder

½ cup (120 ml) heavy cream or whipping cream

1½ cups (360 ml) milk of choice (dairy or nondairy)

Directions

1   Chill a large mixing bowl and hand whisk in the freezer for about 20 minutes.

2   In a separate large bowl, mix the confectioners' sugar and cocoa powder until well combined.

3   Remove the chilled bowl and whisk from the freezer and add the cream into it. Whisk the cream until it starts to thicken. Slowly add the cocoa and sugar mixture to the cream as you continue to whisk.

4   Once the chocolate whipped cream is thick (like a frosting), divide the milk between two glasses (¾ cup, or 180 ml, of milk each) and top with the chocolate whipped cream.

 TIP: To drink cold, serve over ice.

KIWI DELISH SMOOTHIE

 Total Time: 5 minutes

 Makes: 2 servings

Ingredients

3 kiwis

½ green apple, chopped

½ cup (10 g) baby spinach

½ cup (120 ml) cold water

Directions

1 Peel and dice the kiwis.

2 In a blender, add the diced kiwi, apple, spinach, and water and blend until smooth.

3 Pour the smoothie into two glasses and serve.

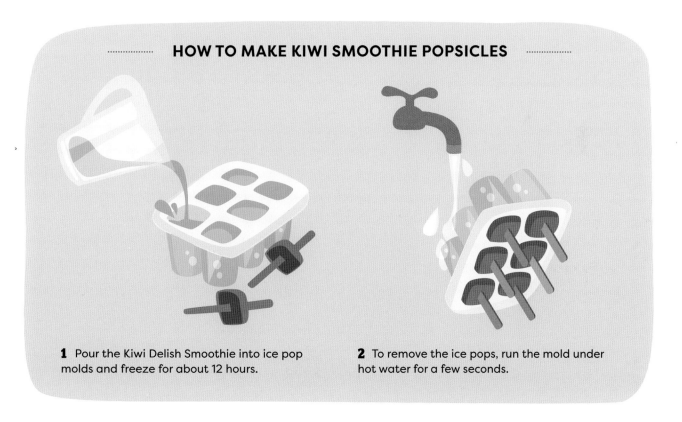

HOW TO MAKE KIWI SMOOTHIE POPSICLES

1 Pour the Kiwi Delish Smoothie into ice pop molds and freeze for about 12 hours.

2 To remove the ice pops, run the mold under hot water for a few seconds.

PARENTS WORKING WITH YOUNGER CHILDREN

If you are a parent who wants to cook with a younger child or your toddler, there are a few things you can do to make some of these recipes more fun and even safer for your kids. Here are a few tips to make sure your toddler can make these recipes with you in a safe and creative way.

1. If you want your young one involved in cutting or slicing some ingredients that you deem are safe, such as some soft fruits, cheese, or dough, you may want to get some toddler kitchen utensils, such as a toddler knife, cut-resistant cooking gloves, and cooking shapes so they can work with tools that they can control and are safe for them to use. You can look online for these items, and they usually come in a bundle and are decently priced.

2. Start out with simpler recipes that may not require any heat. This is a good time to begin teaching them kitchen safety rules, such as not touching the stove (even when it's off), washing hands, not touching adult knives, etc.

3. A toddler can manage simpler cooking steps such as:
   a. Measuring ingredients
   b. Mixing ingredients that you have already measured for them
   c. Pouring liquids or ingredients into bowls and mixers
   d. Helping you wash produce or herbs
   e. Sprinkling seasonings or spices into recipes
   f. Creating shapes out of ingredients such as dough or cookies

4. Make it fun! Let them be as independent as possible when it's safe to do so and guide them when they need it, but let them make mistakes and have fun with the ingredients. Also, let them taste a dish when it's safe to consume so they are trying and enjoying the fruits of their labor. Making food fun also helps picky eaters.

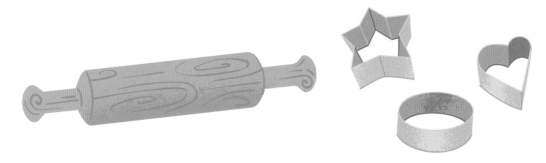

PICKY EATERS

Most of us parents probably have dealt with a picky eater before. It's difficult to get picky eaters to try new foods or to eat their veggies or fruits, but this is where fun cooking comes in! Allowing your children to cook and explore foods without the pressure of eating certain foods helps them have more fun and gives them more incentive to try new foods. Here are some tips to getting your picky eater to try some of the recipes in this book and/or to try new foods.

1. Make cooking a family affair and have them help you with basic tasks (e.g., washing produce, mixing ingredients, making food shapes). This ensures that they will be part of the experience of making their own food and makes it more interesting for them, giving them more of an incentive to try new foods.

2. Make the cooking experience fun! Try different play activities with food while they are cooking in the kitchen (making characters with different ingredients, using the five senses to describe a particular fruit or vegetable, making a rainbow with fruits and vegetables such as on page 50). This again takes the pressure off them feeling like they have to eat, gets them to enjoy whatever they are doing, and gives them more room to try new foods.

3. Add a food item that they know and like to accompany a recipe or the new food that they are trying. This way they have something that they know and feel comfortable with and something new.

4. You can also do something super simple like adding a fruit to their water or making creative smoothies with some greens (e.g., broccoli and spinach) and colorful fruits that they may like (e.g., oranges, bananas, and strawberries).

5. Let them see you (their parent) try the food as well so they can feel comfortable trying it too.

6. Be consistent! Even if they don't want to try new foods, continue to make them a part of the kitchen and add new foods to their plates. Eventually, you will notice a change and they will start opening up to a new food item.

HEALTHY EATING

Food is an essential part of life. It gives your body the nutrients it needs and helps you stay strong and healthy. The food that you eat affects how you feel day to day and your energy to play and think, plus it gives your body and brain the proper fuel they need to function and grow. This is why eating a well-balanced diet is important to your overall growth. A healthy diet helps prevent many chronic illnesses, such as cancer, diabetes, and heart disease. To maintain a healthy diet, it's important to make sure you eat the following food groups every day:

- Vegetables
- Fruits
- Grains
- Protein
- Dairy

The amount you eat for each category depends on your age, weight, sex, height, physical activities, and other factors. You can find out more about what and how much of each food category you can eat by either you and/or your parents talking to your doctor. Or if you want to learn more about healthy eating and what to add to your plate, you can visit https://www.myplate.gov. Here is a list of other essential things you can do to make sure you are maintaining a healthy lifestyle:

- Drink water or 100 percent fresh fruit juice instead of soda or sugary drinks.
- Be active for at least 1 hour a day. This can include taking a walk, playing a sport, dancing, and riding your bike.
- Make sure that the grains you eat are mostly whole grains, as they are much healthier than refined grains.
- Try to eat a variety of fruits and vegetables of different colors, such as dark green, orange, and red.

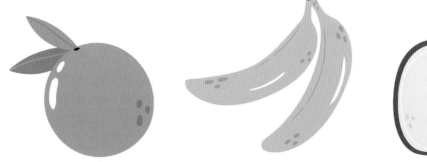

GOOD FOOD CHOICES

Here's a quick chart listing the types of foods in each category. I've also included some measurements of how much you can eat in a day—these are just estimates.

FOOD CATEGORY	EXAMPLES	WHAT YOU CAN EAT
Vegetables	**Dark green:** broccoli, cilantro, mixed greens, romaine lettuce, arugula, kale, spinach **Red and orange:** red and orange bell peppers, butternut squash, red chile peppers, 100 percent vegetable juice, pumpkin, carrots, pimiento, calabaza, sweet potatoes **Starchy veggies:** fufu, breadfruit, plantains, green bananas, white potatoes, cassava, corn, yams, yuca, green beans **Other veggies:** onions, garlic, avocado, celery, beets, cucumbers, Brussels sprouts, radishes, scallions, zucchini, tomatillos, green peppers, seaweed	1 to 2 cups (150 to 300 g)
Legumes	Beans, lentils, pigeon peas, brown peas, pink beans, lima beans, white beans, soy beans, chickpeas (garbanzo beans), pinto beans, edamame	½ cup (90 g)

FOOD CATEGORY	EXAMPLES	WHAT YOU CAN EAT
Fruits	**Berries:** acaí berries, cranberries, blackberries, gooseberries, currants, blueberries, strawberries, raspberries, kiwifruit **100 percent fruit juice:** apple, mango, pomegranate, prune, cranberry, papaya, grape, pineapple **Melons:** cantaloupe, casaba, watermelon, honeydew, horned melon (kiwano) **Other fruits:** apples, bananas, grapefruit, oranges, cherries, apricots, lemons, pears, prunes, star fruit, tangerines, pomegranates, guava, dragon fruit, pineapple, passion fruit, figs, Buddha's hand	½ to 1 cup (75 to 150 g)
Grains	**Whole grains:** popcorn, whole-grain cornmeal, whole wheat cereal flakes, whole wheat sandwich buns and rolls, quinoa, dark rye, whole wheat tortillas, bread, pasta, rolled oats, brown rice **Refined grains:** cornbread, bagels, noodles, white rice, cookies, biscuits, couscous, pancakes, English muffins, pizza crust, white sandwich rolls and buns, waffles, corn tortillas, masa, rice cakes, grits, challah bread	5 to 6 oz (142 to 170 g)

FOOD CATEGORY	EXAMPLES	WHAT YOU CAN EAT
Protein	**Meats:** beef, pork, ham, turkey, venison **Poultry:** chicken, turkey, duck **Fish:** light tuna, snapper, herring, shrimp, octopus, crab, salmon, cod, clams, lobster, sardines **Eggs** **Nuts and seeds:** almonds, peanuts, sunflower seeds, cashews, pumpkin seeds, pecans, peanut butter **Beans, peas, and lentils:** lentils, pigeon beans, chickpeas, pink beans, pinto beans **Soy:** tofu, veggie burgers	4 to 5 oz (113 to 142 g)
Dairy	**Milk:** buttermilk, low-fat (1%) milk, whole milk, flavored milks, reduced-fat (2%) milk, lactose-free milk, frozen yogurt, pudding, smoothies, ice cream **Cheese:** cheddar, Parmesan, American, mozzarella, provolone, Swiss, queso blanco, queso fresco	2 to 2½ cups (480 to 600 g)

DAIRY-, AND GLUTEN-FREE ALTERNATIVES

Some recipes throughout this book include dairy and gluten. Some of the ingredients below may not be listed in the recipes but are good to know about. They can provide necessary nutrients as well.

While I'm providing you with suggestions for alternatives for some dairy- and gluten-free products based on my own research, it is up to you and your family to speak to your doctor to ensure these alternatives are good options for you and your specific dietary needs.

DAIRY-FREE ALTERNATIVES

DAIRY PRODUCT	DAIRY-FREE SUBSTITUTES
Milk	Milk made with: soy, rice, oat, almond, coconut, cashew
Yogurt	Yogurt made with: coconut, soy, almond, hemp
Soft cheese	Hummus, cashew cream cheese, tofu, almond cream cheese, vegan cream cheese
Hard cheese	Nutritional yeast, tofu, nut cheeses
Butter	Nut butters, coconut butter, vegetable oil blends, cultured coconut or cashew vegan butter

GLUTEN-FREE ALTERNATIVES

GLUTEN PRODUCT	GLUTEN-FREE SUBSTITUTES
Bread	Lettuce leaves, cucumber slices, sweet potato slices, rice cakes, gluten-free wraps, corn tortillas, cauliflower bread
Pasta	Pasta made with: rice, corn, buckwheat, amaranth, quinoa, teff, millet, sorghum, lentils, chickpeas, soybeans, cassava, sweet potato, cauliflower
All-purpose flour	Flour made with: almond, buckwheat, sorghum, brown rice, oat, chickpea, coconut
Cereal	Honey Nut Cheerios, Purely Elizabeth Ancient Grain Granola, Barbara's Puffins Honey Rice Cereal, Rice Chex Cereal, Magic Spoon
Soy sauce	Tamari, coconut aminos, Bragg's liquid aminos

INDEX

REFERENCES

Front Matter Sources (pages 10–27)

https://www.marthastewart.com/1112123/your-grocery-list-perfect-pantry-and-how-keep-it-perpetually-stocked

https://www.foodnetwork.com/recipes/packages/cooking-from-the-pantry/pantry-essentials-checklist

https://www.fsis.usda.gov/food-safety/safe-food-handling-and-preparation/food-safety-basics/kitchen-thermometers

https://spendsmart.extension.iastate.edu/spendsmart/2018/02/19/kitchen-safety-knife-safety/

https://www.thekitchn.com/how-to-cut-carrots-194735

https://www.mealpro.net/blog/how-to-cut-vegetables-cutting-guide/#gref

https://www.foodnetwork.com/how-to/articles/knife-skills-101/how-to-dice

https://www.culinaryhill.com/how-to-cut-broccoli/

https://www.healthline.com/nutrition/washing-vegetables#best-methods

https://www.mychicagosteak.com/steak-university/done-perfection-guide-steak-doneness

https://www.sugar.org/sugar/types/

https://www.webstaurantstore.com/article/814/burger-temperature-chart.html

https://www.jessicagavin.com/different-types-of-flour-and-uses/

https://www.tasteofhome.com/article/what-is-cultured-butter/#:~:text=You'll%20likely%20want%20to,flavor%20that%20cultured%20butter%20provides.

https://www.bonappetit.com/story/whats-the-difference-between-regular-cultured-and-european-butter

https://www.vanderbilt.edu/AnS/Chemistry/courses/chem104/experiment1/volumetric/volumetric2.htm#:~:text=The%20Meniscus&text=When%20observing%20a%20volume%20of,liquid%20is%20called%20the%20meniscus.

https://recipes.howstuffworks.com/food-facts/what-is-lemon-zest.htm

Back Matter Sources (pages 180–185)

https://www.tastingtable.com/940897/best-dairy-free-cheese-alternatives/

https://www.cooksmarts.com/articles/gluten-free-diet-substitutions-list/

https://www.healthline.com/nutrition/gluten-free-flours

https://www.myplate.gov/

https://gluten.org/2023/01/23/gluten-free-pasta-fun-new-alternatives/#:~:text=Amaranth%2C%20Quinoa%2C%20Teff%2C%20Millet%2C%20Sorghum&text=You%20may%20discover%20you%20especially,lots%20of%20pasta%20dishes%2C%20too.

https://lowhistamineeats.com/gluten-free-bread-substitutes/

https://www.delish.com/cooking/g19422633/gluten-free-cereal/

https://www.bhg.com/recipes/desserts/cookies/gluten-free-cookie-recipes/

Sidebar Pages Sources (Pages 40–41, 60–61, 72–73, 112–113, 144–145, 162–163)

https://dailyhive.com/montreal/montreal-bagel-space

https://www.eatthis.com/bagel-facts/

https://www.cbc.ca/news/canada/montreal/what-the-montreal-behind-the-montreal-bagel-1.5226630#:~:text=The%20bagel%20originated%20in%20Poland,Jewish%20immigrants%20coming%20to%20Canada.

https://www.theatlantic.com/health/archive/2009/03/the-secret-history-of-bagels/6928/

https://chompies.com/a-delicious-history-of-the-bagel-in-america/#:~:text=Bagels%20arrived%20in%20the%20United,enjoy%20them%20on%20the%20street.

https://www.tastingtable.com/1000518/the-migratory-history-of-the-empanada/

https://www.elsursf.com/news-item/a-brief-history-of-empanadas/

https://www.delish.com/kitchen-tools/g40818614/types-of-cheese/

https://www.eat-japan.com/sushi-perfect/sushi-knwoledge/sushi-history/

https://www.history.com/topics/ancient-americas/history-of-chocolate

https://candyusa.com/story-of-chocolate/fun-facts-about-chocolate/

https://www.smithsonianmag.com/history/unusual-origins-pink-lemonade-180960145/#:~:text=Allott%20%2C%20a%20Chicago%20native%20who,pink%2Dhued%20beverage%20as%20is.

Fun Facts Sources (pages 43, 53, 116, 127)

https://mobile-cuisine.com/did-you-know/muffin-fun-facts/#:~:text=English%20muffins%20which%20are%20yeast,end%20of%20the%2018th%20century.

https://www.rosiesworld.co.nz/all-about-dairy/dairy-goodness/yoghurt/#:~:text=Yoghurt%20is%20one%20of%20nature's,the%20Middle%20Eastern%20country%20Turkey.

https://snakeriverseeds.com/blogs/news/5-fun-facts-about-carrots-that-will-make-you-more-interesting-at-parties

https://www.almanac.com/sweet-potato-facts-and-benefits

How To Source (page 50)

https://www.bonappetit.com/test-kitchen/how-to-cut-a-pineapple

THANK YOU

To my children who gave me life.

To MJ for always encouraging me.

To my parents for always supporting my dreams.

To my siblings for always cheering me on.

To my friends and family for celebrating with me.

To my online familia—for joining me on this journey and letting me inspire you.

THANK YOU ALL.

ABOUT THE AUTHOR

Rossini Perez is a foodie and mother who combines her love for her daughter and love of food to create her own unique kid- and family-friendly meals. She is bilingual (English and Spanish) and has gained an online following because of her creative, fun, and healthy lunch ideas. She has a large and dedicated following who eagerly watch and share her cooking and lunch videos. Follow her on TikTok (@ross_ini), Instagram (@tinatakeslunch and @ross_ini), and YouTube @RossiniPerez.

First published in 2024 by Rock Point, an imprint of The Quarto Group,
142 West 36th Street, 4th Floor, New York, NY 10018, USA
(212) 779-4972 www.Quarto.com

Rock Point titles are also available at discount for retail, wholesale, promotional, and bulk purchase.
For details, contact the Special Sales Manager by email at specialsales@quarto.com or by mail
at The Quarto Group, Attn: Special Sales Manager, 100 Cummings Center Suite 265D, Beverly, MA
01915 USA.

10 9 8 7 6 5 4 3 2 1

ISBN: 978-1-63106-949-9

Digital edition published in 2024
eISBN: 978-0-7603-8301-8

Library of Congress Control Number: 2023945000

Group Publisher: Rage Kindelsperger
Editorial Director: Erin Canning
Creative Director: Laura Drew
Senior Art Director: Marisa Kwek
Managing Editor: Cara Donaldson
Editor: Keyla Pizarro-Hernández
Cover Design: Marisa Kwek
Interior Layout: Kim Winscher
Photography: Erin Scott
Food Styling: Lillian Kang
Food Styling Assistant: Paige Arnett

Printed in China

All activities in this book should be performed with adult supervision. The publisher and authors do not
assume any responsibility for damages or injuries resulting from any activities.